EDDIE COCHRAN
In person!

**Dedicated to Pavlos,
George and Andreas**

*Eddie Cochran was the best rock star ever.
He played great, he looked great, he wrote great songs
and he was an innovator in the studio.
Anyone who wants to be a rock'n'roller has
to be hip to Eddie Cochran.*

Slim Jim Phantom,
Los Angeles, January 2023

Copyright © 2023 Omnibus Press
(A division of the Wise Music Group,
14–15 Berners Street, London, W1T 3LJ)

Design by Lora Findlay

ISBN 978-1-9131-7296-1

Lee Bullman hereby asserts his right to be identified as the author of this work
in accordance with Sections 77 to 78 of the Copyright, Designs and Patents Act 1988.

All rights reserved. No part of this book may be reproduced in any form
or by any electronic or mechanical means, including information storage or
retrieval systems, without permission in writing from the publisher,
except by a reviewer who may quote brief passages.

Every effort has been made to trace the copyright holders of the
photographs in this book but one or two were unreachable. We would be
grateful if the photographers concerned would contact us.

A catalogue record for this book is available from the British Library.

Printed in the Czech Republic.

Find out more about the Eddie Cochran: The Lost Locker Collection online at
killertonerecords.co.uk

www.omnibuspress.com

EDDIE COCHRAN
In person!

Lee Bullman

Introduction

THIS COLLECTION OF Eddie Cochran's personal possessions was almost lost forever. Decades after his untimely death, when the Cochran family home was sold, Eddie's possessions wound up in a storage facility. In 2021, when the rent on the facility had lapsed and the storage company needed to recoup their money, the locker containing Eddie's possessions was offered up for sale. No one knew what treasures were hidden inside. The Pasadena antiques dealer who bought the locker did so blind, and only on inspecting it did he realise what he had. He'd bought Eddie's records, unfinished songs, clothes and family photos. In fact, the antiques dealer had bought a snapshot of Eddie's life, perfectly preserved by Eddie's doting mother Alice and sister Gloria throughout their lifetimes. He'd bought us all an insight into who Eddie was; a glimpse of the young man behind the iconic silhouette, the half-smile and the perfect rock'n'roll.

When Eddie died, his family, traumatised, shocked and heartbroken by their loss, turned his bedroom into a shrine. It remained as it had on the day he left in early 1960 to fly into London and became somewhere the family could go to try to make sense of their grief. The collection found in that bedroom illuminates a journey through hope, success and tragedy. It reminds us how young Eddie was, and reminds us of his immense talent. It also shows us things we might not have seen before. We get a sense of Eddie's sense of humour, his dedication to rock'n'roll and the short but incredible journey that dedication took him on. It shows us Eddie working hard and having fun, and that music and family came first. Eddie Cochran was lightning in a bottle; his story is the original rock'n'roll story. It tells us how Eddie became a legend whilst keeping his feet on the ground and his priorities straight. The collection gets us close to Eddie, so close that we get a real sense of him, of what he was like and what he liked, where he'd been and where he was at. There are, of course, questions the collection doesn't answer. It doesn't tell us what Eddie would have gone on to do, it doesn't play us the music he would have made or show us the career he could have had, but it gives us somewhere to bring our dreams of Eddie Cochran back to life.

On the south coast of England, there is a house overlooking the sea. There's a 1964 Mustang parked on one side of the drive and a pink and chrome Cadillac parked on the other. The house is home to Sonny West; musician, self-made man, devoted father of three, creative maverick and dyed-in-the-wool rock'n'roll rebel. Sonny's not your average guy, so when the stars aligned and Sonny got the chance to acquire the Eddie Cochran collection, he did so without missing a beat. Sonny noticed that Eddie's possessions were being offered for sale one by one and that the collection was being broken up and sold as individual items, so he bought everything he could and had it shipped to the UK. With a little help from his friends, Sonny started unboxing, cataloguing and archiving. Sonny West's Eddie Cochran Collection is a dizzying assemblage of Eddie's personal possessions and unique pieces of memorabilia. There are pieces of Eddie's clothing, such as a hand-tooled brown leather belt and matching buckle. There are cheques which Eddie wrote and notes and dedications from Eddie's rock'n'roll contemporaries – Gene Vincent, the Everly Brothers and Little Richard all wrote to him. There are photographs that no one has ever seen before where another side of Eddie emerges; the original oil painting that graced his album covers; the bag of hundreds of fan club pins, and the love his fans had for him pouring from the stack of letters they sent. There are also records; Eddie's personal collection of 45s, some by his friends, some by his labelmates and some by his heroes.

There are a few things you need to know about Sonny West and why he is the reason this collection exists. You need to know that from the age of 8, rock'n'roll was instilled and ingrained in him. You need to know that Sonny's dad, a Teddy Boy from before they had a name for them, used to let Sonny skip school and go to work with him on his lorry. The lorry didn't have a radio so Sonny's dad would get him to sing on the road. He'd sing the music he heard at home, the music his dad played: Johnny Cash, early rock'n'roll, Chuck Berry. Sonny dug Chuck Berry the most from early on, when he was 9 years old and his dad took him to see Chuck live. Chuck was on form that night and Sonny was hooked.

At 14 years old, Sonny was still finding his way in the world and the options for a kid from a rural, working-class background didn't look great. He'd been getting tattooed since he was 12 and had pretty much given up on school, just like school had given up on him. Sonny's upbringing gave him some valuable skills; he was a keen shot and owned his own rifles, he was a respected amateur boxer and was headed for a career in the Royal Marines. Sonny was good with motorcycles, so good that he was trading them, fixing them up and riding them to school. He rode them to school on the days he bothered to go. Sonny fixed a BSA Bantam that he decided to make his daily rider. That meant he could get rid of the fizzy Suzuki he'd fixed up when he was 13, so he traded it for something which caught his eye at a friend's house, something that spoke to him and pulled him in... a guitar.

Sonny West – keeping the flame alive.

The guitar Sonny swapped for the Suzuki was a 1959 blonde Harmony Meteor and it caused problems immediately. The parents of the guy Sonny did the deal with weren't happy and it looked for a while like the trade might not happen. But it did. So he took it home and put on some of his dad's records and started trying to play along. It took a while because anything worth doing does, but the more Sonny played along to those records the more he started to sound like them. Sonny was picking crops and doing farm labour; jobs he'd had to take since he left school. His nights were spent trying to find the notes, the chords, the riffs, tracking them down one by one. He applied the work ethic instilled in him to mastering the guitar and in the process he opened up a whole other world. Sonny spent hours, days and weeks diligently mastering the riffs from the tunes he'd sung along to in his dad's truck until he got better. Then, he got good.

There weren't many rockers around where Sonny grew up, so he started poring over the music press, reading about its movers and shakers, pressing his face up against a window to the world he could feel, but couldn't quite touch. The back pages of *Melody Maker*, *Sounds* and the *NME* carried ads for mail-order Bowie trousers and gig listings alongside a Musicians Wanted section and Sonny read it all. One week, there was an ad that caught his eye. It was for a gig in London's West End Theatreland. They were putting on a show called *Forever Elvis* and they wanted to do it with a live band. There were auditions, so Sonny applied. At 16, he was too young to care that he didn't have any experience or that there were thousands of established guitar players out there – he had nothing to lose. So, Sonny got to the audition and stood in front of the producers. They asked him to play along to Elvis' Sun recordings, the very songs he'd been devoting his nights to ever since he got the Harmony Meteor. Sonny knew them note for note, he'd got the nuances down, he instinctively had the sound and he looked the part, so they gave him the role and saved him from boredom, prison and other trouble. Sixteen-year-old Sonny didn't know it, but rock'n'roll had just saved his soul.

Fast forward to right here, right now and Sonny West has played on stages all over the world with some of the most iconic names in rock'n'roll. His time in the Elvis show led him to perform with the Jordinnaires and Scotty Moore, bona fide architects of the rock'n'roll sound. He's been in bands, become a successful musician and songwriter, has records with his name on them and has a collection of vintage guitars that feels like a hip museum. Now he has gathered together the physical fragments of an icon's life, the echoes of a hero, and kept them together, where they belong.

Sonny believes that 'even though I tracked down every item in the collection and it wouldn't exist without me, and even though I had it all shipped, catalogued and photographed, framed, it doesn't feel as though I own it. It feels like I'm in charge of it for a while, looking after it for Eddie and for us all.'

Contents

Introduction **5**

Part One
From Albert Lea to Bristol **9**

Part Two
Afterwards **161**

Part Three
Where Are They Now? **179**

Acknowledgements **189**

Like father, like son. Frank and Eddie.

Chapter One

IN AMERICA'S MIDWEST, around an hour and a half south of Minnesota's twin cities at the junction of Interstates 90 and 35, lies the small town of Albert Lea. You can feel the seasons pass in Albert Lea, the summers blaze hot there and the winters put a chill in you so deep you'll think it'll never leave. The town was built from the dirt up. Its first single cabin was erected in 1855 but such was its popularity amongst settlers that it grew to need its own schoolhouse just two years later.

Albert Lea began its life as a farming and manufacturing town but by 1938 it was, as were many similar towns all over America, quietly suffering. There was no water, crops were sparse and times were hard. By then the town's population had reached twelve thousand, a lot of mouths to feed when food and work were thin on the ground. The Wall Street crash of 1929 and the ensuing depression had cast a long, dark shadow over towns like Albert Lea. There were rays of hope, though. Stars had started falling to Earth and in 1938 there were children being born all over America who would go on to leave the world a very different place from the one they found. Bill Withers and Ben E King were born in 1938. So were Evel Knievel, Nico and JJ Cale.

One of Albert Lea's inhabitants, Frank Cochran, was a strong, quiet, hardworking man. A Navy veteran, Frank had brought his family to Albert Lea for the only reason anyone seemed to go anywhere in those days, to find work. Now, more than ever, Frank needed a steady, decent paying job. He had a houseful of kids already, and there was another on the way in the fall. On 3 October 1938, Frank's wife Alice gave birth to a son, the couple's fifth child. They named the boy Ray Edward Cochran. The world would come to know him as Eddie.

Eddie Cochran was born into a world of love. His four older siblings, Gloria, Bill, Bob and Patricia, were delighted by the arrival of their newest, littlest brother and took turns pitching in and helping Alice take care of him. Photographs of the Cochrans back then show a close family making the best of what were at times, difficult circumstances. Eddie's introduction to music came early; as an infant he would fall happily to sleep with his thumb in his mouth listening to brother Bill playing 78s on the family record player. What the Cochrans lacked in material wealth, they more than made up for at home with a warm, loving environment created, maintained and overseen by Alice. Eddie could do no wrong in his mother's eyes, their bond was tight. Alice adored her youngest boy. The pair shared jokes and nicknames, Eddie called her 'Shrimper', and between them they created a world that excluded all others. Eddie's hunting trips with his brothers around Albert Lea inspired his life-long love of outdoor pursuits, particularly those which involved shooting. On one trip with brother Bob, Eddie accidentally took a .22 to the leg after a mishap with his rifle. Luckily, Shrimper was away with Frank in Oklahoma, so the Cochran siblings figured they could keep the incident from her and shield themselves from her wrath. No such luck. Alice knew her kids better than they knew themselves and saw straight through the plot to keep her in the dark, and she wasn't happy about it at all.

Eddie's childhood passed like many did in Albert Lea, indeed like many all over rural and semi-rural America. There were lots of other kids around and Eddie found his first tribe when he befriended a couple of local boys, David Lindahl and Terry Cole. Eddie had had his own gun since he was young, a fancy western style BB rifle, and liked nothing better than hunting, shooting or fishing with his brothers or David and Terry. According to Terry's recollection, David was the son of the local sheriff which meant that when it was free of drunks, thieves, brawlers and conmen, Eddie and his friends had the local jail as their playground where they could add a touch of cell door reality to their games of cops and robbers or Eddie's favourite, cowboys and Indians. An early picture of Eddie captures him pistol drawn, dressed head to toe in western wear with a double buckle belt on his holster and a neckerchief and ten-gallon hat to complete the look. Westerns were huge when Eddie was growing up, he loved Tom Mix, Gene Autry and Hopalong Cassidy. Aspects of the cowboy movies were familiar to him, it was no wonder he connected with them. He was being raised against the backdrop of a prairie landscape, where land was still used for cattle and where the romantic, endless, wide-open skies of American cowboy culture were what the young Eddie Cochran saw every time he looked up towards the heavens.

Eddie's older brother Bill could have had no idea what he was kickstarting when he went and bought himself a Kay guitar. Kay guitars weren't the best on the market by any means, but the company was known for making reliable, serviceable instruments for the musician on a budget. When Bill went away to serve in the military the guitar remained behind, forgotten for a while, gathering dust in a cupboard in the family home.

Brother Bill had shown Eddie a couple of chords on the Kay but at that point his musical ambition was drawing him toward the beat, and he decided to learn the drums. When he was told that in order to play the drums he'd first have to spend time learning the piano, Eddie suddenly wasn't so keen. He kept on with his quest to find something to play and tried the trombone for a while, then, at a teacher's suggestion, considered the clarinet.

(Left) Eddie, Frank and Shrimper.

Again, no joy. Eddie could get a tune out of pretty much anything but none of the instruments he was trying were sitting quite right with him, so he turned his attention back to that Kay guitar of brother Bill's in the cupboard at home. He retrieved the guitar and got brother Bob to help him get started on it. Bob showed Eddie around the thing and taught him the basics and either at that moment or at some point soon after, Eddie Cochran fell in love with the six-string guitar. When he wasn't cleaning the Kay he was playing it. Eddie got hold of the *Complete Chord and Harmony Manual for Guitar* and a bunch more guitar how-to's and manuals and he practised, practised, practised.

Around him, things were changing in the Cochran household. Eddie grew up in a hectic home full of siblings and laughter and squabbles and noise but the place was starting to empty as, one by one, Eddie's older brothers and sisters were flying the nest and starting their own lives and families. Bob, Bill and Gloria had all gotten married and the place had quietened down. Eddie filled the new silence at home with the sound of the Kay guitar. The longer he spent sitting on the edge of his bed or on the couch with that guitar, the more comfortable he got with it. By the time he saw that all the late nights and long afternoons with the Kay were starting to pay off, that it was starting to sound how he wanted and give voice to something within, he was utterly hooked. It took a little while, but Eddie proved to be a natural.

While Eddie was practising, his dad Frank was planning the family's next move. Once again motivated by the need to earn, Frank Cochran announced that he, Alice and Eddie were moving to Oklahoma where Frank would find gainful employment at a local Air Force base. The small band of Cochrans packed up and drove the 700 miles to their new home, but once they arrived it soon became apparent that they wouldn't be staying for long. Alice missed being near her other kids and with no warning, Eddie fell suddenly and seriously ill. Though details about the illness are sketchy, we do know that Eddie's sickness was most likely a kidney problem and that it scared the whole family. The Cochrans were tight, the crisis with Eddie reminded them just how tight, and it wasn't long before the move to Oklahoma was abandoned and Frank, Alice and Eddie loaded up their possessions and drove from sunrise 'til sunset, back to Albert Lea.

The return home, if that's what it was, was not to last for long. Brother Bill kept calling from California where he was serving in the Navy and attached to the Marines. Service in the Navy was becoming something of a Cochran family tradition. Brother Bob had followed in Frank's footsteps and had enlisted in the Navy too. Brother Bill was adamant that the family should join he and his wife Betty out in California where there was sunshine and work. The Cochrans were used to moving around and didn't take much convincing. Once again, they packed everything they had into a couple of beat-up cars and drove nearly two thousand miles out to California.

(Left) sharp shooter.

(This page) All-American boy, at home with the Cochrans. Clockwise: Eddie, Shrimper and Patty; Eddie, Patty and Bobby; Eddie; Winter in Albert Lea.

Under Shrimper's ever-watchful eye, Eddie and his siblings grew up in a household filled with fun, noise and love.

A military background: Eddie in uniform.

California, here we come.

Chapter Two

EDDIE'S LIFE CHANGED with that 1951 drive out to California. He spent the journey to The Golden State clutching, strumming and cleaning his guitar on the backseat of the jalopy. When Shrimper referred to the guitar as a possession Eddie corrected her and told his mama it was his best friend. The California they arrived in was a world away from Oklahoma and Albert Lea, the culture that Eddie found himself surrounded by couldn't have been more different than that which he'd left behind only days before. California was diverse and surprising, the sun shone every day and everything was just that little bit looser, a little more prosperous and optimistic. The dustbowl workwear and pick-up trucks of wide open America were suddenly replaced by bikinis and convertibles. Hollywood was the centre of the movie industry, Los Angeles was a magnet, every day would-be stars were arriving there from all over with a one-way ticket and a dream. When the family first got to the West Coast they moved in with brother Bill for a while, then set up home in a haphazard succession of unsatisfactory temporary accommodation until the Cochrans finally found a house where they could spend some time and settle for a while, at 5539 Priory Street.

In September 1951, Eddie enrolled at the local school, Bell Gardens Junior High, and wasn't there long before he crossed paths with another student, the double bass player in the school orchestra, Fred Conrad Smith. Fred would go on to obtain a nickname that would stick a few years later, when everyone started calling him Guybo. Like Eddie, Guybo was a talented music obsessive with a good sense of humour, so almost inevitably, the two soon became fast friends and spent as much time as they could jamming together. Guybo's love of music was evidenced by his feel for it. Something about the bass resonated with him and pretty soon he was starting to stroll through tunes at the bottom end and put some Guybo swing into everything they played together. The jam sessions would take place at Eddie's house under the proud and watchful gaze of Queen Alice. Occasionally, other kids would join the sessions and play along for a while and try to keep up, but they all dropped out eventually. Eddie and Guybo kept on jamming. They were in it for the long haul and would remain friends forever.

Eddie Cochran was an inquisitive, smart and confident kid. Aside from this growing interest in music, his energy and inquisitiveness led him to experiment in other extracurricular areas too. He worked as editor-in-chief of the school paper and played an active role in Student Court. It was becoming clear to everybody around him though that no matter what Eddie did or where Eddie went, he always came back to music. It was his first love, and he'd fallen deep. To indulge this love, Eddie and Guybo hooked up with another Bell Gardens Junior High student, Al Garcia, and formed their first band. They settled on the name The Melodie Boys and set to rehearsing. By now Eddie had opened up a whole new world of sound, he'd upgraded from Bill's old Kay guitar and got himself a Gibson and added a DeArmond pickup. It was a big step up, good guitars weren't cheap and soon The Melodie Boys got to the point where they were ready to try out in front of a live audience, to deliver the 'Western rhythms, Dance and Cowboy Ballads' promised on their business card, and so they booked their first gig.

As the spring of 1953 turned into summer, Eddie was starting to feel at home amongst local musicians and began hanging out with them every chance he got, so it wasn't long before he met Chuck. Chuck Foreman was 19, he was five years older than Eddie, but he took the kid seriously on account of his obvious talent, his easy-going nature and his unremitting drive. Chuck, a respected steel player in his own right, noted Eddie's musical ear early on, his ability to hear a tune and remember it, then sit down, work it out and play it. Chuck had high standards when it came to music and musicians and he recognised early on that Eddie was aiming for something higher too. Crucially, Chuck Foreman was in possession of a two-track tape-recorder, cutting-edge, state of the art technology in the mid-fifties. Two tracks meant that Chuck and Eddie could record a backing track then play along to it and record the result.

Chuck's two-track set-up was Eddie Cochran's introduction to the possibilities of recorded sound. Suddenly a tune wasn't something that was played once and gone but instead something that could be laboured over, experimented with, improved, transformed. Sadly, although Eddie and Chuck had the ability to record two tracks, the tape on which to record them was expensive and hard to come by, so many of those early experimental sessions were recorded over time and again in a search for the sounds they could hear in their heads. Though simple by today's standards, this method of recording was blazing a trail. Overdubbing, the technical name for the process of laying tracks on top of one another, would become an integral part of Eddie's approach in the studio. Once exposed to it, Eddie eagerly embraced the potential of the new studio technology while many other musicians were still convinced it would put them out of work. Up to that point, records had been produced by assembling musicians, having them perform together live and recording the whole thing, there and then, live in the studio. To the doubters, the new recording technology meant that a single person could replace a whole band, that they could record every instrument one at a time and thereby lose a whole bunch of musicians the wages they'd make on a session. Eddie got it though, he was way ahead of the naysayers. Eddie knew that used correctly the studio wouldn't put bands out of business, it would make them sound better, it would allow them a wider palette from which to paint, and he knew it was the future. Eddie approached the recording process like he approached the guitar, spending as much time as he could around it and endeavouring to master it. On the tracks that do remain recorded by Eddie and Chuck, such as Gambler's Guitar, Eddie can be heard enjoying himself.

Between late '53 and early '54, Eddie was racking up experience wherever he could get it, be that recording with Chuck or playing with local bands and musicians. When he wasn't working with Chuck or jamming with Al and Guybo, he'd go wherever, whenever to jam with other musicians and hone his craft. It was doing him good, this constant exercising of his talent. His skill, feel and confidence were growing and no-one around Eddie at the time could deny that he was getting better fast. Soon he was no longer just playing rhythm, he was learning licks and riffs from Chuck and the other musicians he was playing with and his repertoire was growing. It was around this time that Eddie got his first girlfriend, Johnnie Berry. Johnnie was cool, she understood from the get-go that where Eddie was concerned, the best she could hope for was second place in his affections, just behind the music. Johnnie would hang out while Chuck and Eddie jammed together or experimented with home-made reverb, she'd go out on double dates with Eddie, Chuck and his latest girl in the black 1942 Oldsmobile that Chuck was driving back then. Johnnie and Eddie spent a lot of time on the backseat of Chuck's Oldsmobile, covering whatever might have been going on with the blue suede jacket Eddie wore. Although still only 15, Eddie could more than hold his own amongst older musicians and was soaking up their world like a sponge. He was finding his feet and making it up as he went along, going where his talent and his intuition took him and taking every opportunity that presented itself to make and record music, arriving early, leaving late.

If you played an instrument in Bell Gardens back then, at some point you'd pass through the Bell Gardens Music Centre. The scene at the Music Centre was vibrant and alive, walking in for the first time might have been intimidating but for anyone interested in music, it was the place to be. Like-minded local musicians congregated and hung out there, they wrote songs, formed bands, rehearsed and recorded there. Eddie started showing up every chance he got, expanding his knowledge and his circle of fellow players. It was at the Music Centre that Eddie met Ron Wilson who then introduced him to Warren Flock. Along with Dave Kohrman on bass, Warren and Eddie formed Eddie's next band, The Bell Gardens Ranch Gang. The band did pretty good all things considered, they played some live shows where they were accompanied by a fiddle player and second guitarist and even got on local TV and radio. As always, Eddie was the youngest member of the band, this time by four years, but he managed to more than hold his own for the short time that they stayed together.

Eddie's exposure to media and celebrity began with those fleeting local radio and TV spots. It started small and slow but would eventually build to the point that when the hit records started, he was ready. Cameras didn't scare Eddie, he was shrewd enough to know, even as a young teenager, that it took more than just musical chops to make it and soon became a dab hand at interviews where he came across as natural and enthusiastic and where, if you looked hard enough, you could see that twinkle in his eye. Eddie didn't know it, but he'd started collecting all the skills he needed to become a rock'n'roll star.

In the autumn of 1954, Richard Rae and the Shamrock Valley Boys passed through town for their show at the American Legion Club. The Valley Boys were known for Western Swing, moonshine party music and singalong classics and had earned a decent reputation by the time they played the Legion. Eddie and Chuck got hired to keep the crowd entertained while the band took a beer and bathroom break in their set, and the pair put on such a dynamic performance that they caught the attention of Shamrock Valley Boys' guitar player, Bob Denton. Bob told Eddie about his namesake, Hank Cochran, who played with the Valley Boys occasionally. Hank's real name was Garland Perry Cochran. He'd run away from an orphanage as a kid and learnt guitar from his uncle. Hank had a decent voice and a knowledge of country music so deep that he could take random requests from the audience and play them and sing them like he wrote them. Hank was a purist when it came to his country music, expanding the boundaries and experimenting with the form weren't for him, whereas the Shamrock Valley Boys liked to get a bit raucous and play a bit more fast and loose with traditional tunes, for their own entertainment as much as that of the audience.

For a while, Eddie managed to juggle his schooling and his burgeoning musical career. His junior high grades in the June of '54 were more than respectable and he scored well in Music and English. But Eddie was seeing too much, learning too much and having too much fun outside of school. The muse was calling to him. What started as a hobby had become an obsession and the young Eddie Cochran wanted to turn it into a career. Eddie hooked up with the guy Bob Denton had told him about and when they got together, Hank Cochran was so impressed by Eddie's playing that he asked him to play lead guitar for him. Eddie liked the offer and took it as another sign that in the school and music balance, something was going to have to give. So, in January of '55, Eddie went all in and sold his soul to music, he took a leap of faith and he quit school. Although the Cochran household had always been encouraging and proud of Eddie's musical talent and drive, leaving school seemed like a big move, particularly so close to graduation. Eddie was set on it though, he'd found his world, and now he was going to live in it.

Eddie aged 15, on the baseball field at Bell Gardens Junior High.

Eddie Garland's Country Gentlemen at the American Legion in Bell Gardens. Eddie Garland was an alias for Eddie himself.

Chapter Three

HANK COCHRAN WAS three years older than Eddie. The story was he'd learned to play the guitar while he hitch-hiked with his uncle Otis all the way from Mississippi to the New Mexico oilfields. Eddie and Hank may have not been related but they were more than happy to play along and capitalise on their shared surname by forming The Cochran Brothers, slipstreaming in behind a bunch of established family country acts such as The Louvin Brothers. They started out covering Hank's beloved country standards, tunes guaranteed to raise a smile or a tear by artists like Hank Williams and Ernest Tubb. Soon though, they began to write together and come up with their own material, all heavily influenced by Hank's love of country music and the classics they'd been playing together. It wasn't long before offers of gigs came in and The Cochran Brothers took every one they got. Hank and Eddie worked together well, they gelled on stage and won over audiences. Compared to Eddie, Hank was an old hand in the business but once again, 16-year-old Eddie didn't let his age or inexperience get in the way of his musical ambition. The Cochran Brothers dressed fancy, they took their lead from the rhinestone regalia sported by the western big bands. They wore matching western suits, maverick ties and pearl-poppered shirts. For some extra sparkle, Eddie's sister Gloria sewed lines of sequins up the outsides of their pant legs. Eddie was now playing all the time, he was getting a lot of use out of his trusty Gibson, but there was a guitar he wanted, a guitar he'd seen up close at the Music Centre, a guitar designed and played by his hero Chet Atkins. Eddie idolised Chet, he'd spent hours listening to his records and attempting to replicate what he heard with more and more success. The guitar Eddie wanted was called the 6120, it was the Chet Atkins signature model, and it was made by Gretsch.

That 1955 Gretsch 6120 was a show in and of itself. It came in vibrant orange with brass western appointments, elegant, swooping f-holes, the Gretsch logo branded into its top left corner and a Chet Atkins autographed pickguard in gold. Nothing that beautifully and practically designed, that fragile and indestructible, could sound anything less than amazing. The 6120 was top of the line. When you pulled out a guitar like that, people were going to expect that you could play it. It was a big statement.

Eddie liked the way the 6120 looked, he liked the way it felt, but mostly Eddie liked the way it sounded. There were other good guitars around but the Gretsch could play soft and seductive or it could howl, growl and twang. He could pick at it or strum it. It could shout and it could whisper, its notes could bend, sustain and contort, it had everything he needed. The natural spot for Eddie to acquire his 6120 was the Bell Gardens Music Centre. A brand new Gretsch was a big purchase, getting on for four hundred bucks, way more money than Eddie could pull out of his wallet, so he copped it on a payment plan with some help from his folks and smiled all the way home.

The guitar that Eddie bought from Bell Gardens Music Centre that day would go on to become one of the most iconic instruments in all of rock'n'roll, so it is perhaps fitting that there is a layer of mystery swirling around its origins. The most oft-told story has it that prior to Eddie getting the 6120, local musician Gary Lambert had the guitar as a loaner while his own Gretsch Country Club underwent some bespoke fancification. Eddie's nephew Bobby would later go on to claim that Gary's loaner was a different Gretsch entirely. Whatever the truth of where it had been, it was now exactly where it should be and from that point on, Eddie Cochran and his Gretsch 6120 became synonymous. Hank Cochran recalled that Eddie was rarely seen without the guitar from the moment he bought it. When he bought it, Eddie's guitar was stock, and Eddie was anything but, so he made a couple of modifications to the 6120 that made it his very own. He covered Chet's name in tape on the pickguard then had one of the pickups changed to a Gibson P-90, as favoured by Elvis's guitarist, Scotty Moore. It was while he was having the pickup changed that Eddie had the taped-up pickguard removed from the guitar and replaced with one in clear plastic. The guitar had cost a bunch already, the Bell Gardens receipt Eddie signed on 4 April shows that he spent another fifty dollars on it that day to make it perfect. Once Eddie had made the changes that turned his 6120 into a rock'n'roll icon, he began to do the same with his own image. He started greasing his hair back higher and tighter and he got lucky, he had the perfect hair for a quiff, he started dressing more rock'n'roll, more R'n'B, and he got lucky, everything looked good on him.

Eddie and Hank built up their live chops together to the point where they were spending Friday and Saturday nights playing to a thousand plus people. They'd show up together in Baldwin Park, at the Country Barn Dance, where they'd get up and play, sometimes catching the act of a songwriter who'd perform there occasionally, a guy by the name of Jerry Capehart. Eddie was getting very used to stepping out on stage, he was getting used to being the youngest up there. He was getting used to the girls in the audience gravitating toward him, he was getting used to the lights, getting used to all the attention and the applause. At Cochran Brothers' shows, Hank sang and played while Eddie accompanied him, hanging back for the moment, for the most part behind his Gibson, then behind his Gretsch, happy to let most of the spotlight fall on Hank. They favoured up-tempo numbers that went down a storm live and soon secured the services of a booker, American Music Corporation, which meant that suddenly, someone else was booking all of their gigs, and they were getting way more of them. American Music found them two local TV spots, one on the Town Hall Party, and the other on the Hometown Jamboree where Eddie got another early taste of the media spotlight. Through all of this activity, Eddie was starting to rub shoulders with established and successful musicians, sharing the bill on Town Hall Party with Tex Ritter and Merle Travis. Steve Stebbins, who ran the booking agency, also managed to hook The Cochran Brothers up with the chance to audition for Ekko Records.

Ekko's main office in Memphis was on the same street as Sun Records, their California office was situated at 4949 Hollywood Boulevard. By the time The Cochran Brothers dealt with them, Ekko Records was building up an impressive catalogue of western swing and trad country. The label saw enough promise in The Cochran Brothers to send them down to Western Recorders Studio in Hollywood to record four songs. They got two singles out of the session. The first that was picked for release was on 5 May, 'Mr. Fiddle', with 'Two Blue Singin' Stars' on the flipside. 'Two Blue Singin' Stars' was a tune written by Red Matthews about Hank Williams and Jimmie Rodgers, country icons singing for the pleasure of the folks up in heaven. It was Eddie's first death song, an ode to the departed from those left behind, a format that he would later return to when he would use someone else's song in order to process his own, very real, grief. The song was pure high lonesome country, Hank's sweet spot, it garnered critical accolades but sales were disappointing. Nonetheless Ekko decided to try again with The Cochran Brothers and released 'Guilty Conscience' backed with 'Your Tomorrow Never Comes'. 'Guilty Conscience' didn't do so well either. Within the dynamic of The Cochran Brothers, Hank was far more attached to traditional country than Eddie, even though at that point the audience for the genre was shrinking and what audience there was already served by more than enough established names. People were looking for something new. So was Eddie.

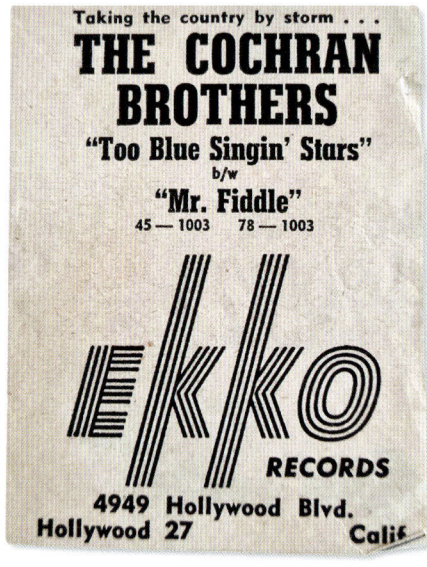

Even though the singles had failed to chart, just releasing them gave Hank and Eddie a boost and set them apart from their immediate contemporaries. They took on a manager, Red Matthews, who headed up the sales and distribution arm of Ekko Records as well as being its A&R man, and gigged and gigged and gigged, scoring another TV appearance in Dallas when they were featured on the *Big D Jamboree*. Although not on the level of the *Grand Ole Opry*, the *Jamboree* could still attract stars like Hank Snow and was one of the first shows to feature a new, young talent from Memphis by the name of Elvis Presley. Eddie and Hank were booked to play the show less than a week after one of Elvis's appearances and heard first hand reports of the chaos his performance of 'That's All Right' had inspired. The crowd had gone wild, girls had grabbed at the singer and torn his clothes, a policeman had been injured trying to protect him. Right in front of Eddie Cochran's eyes, within touching distance, rock'n'roll was being born and Elvis Presley was just starting to ride the wave that would carry him all the way to stardom and beyond. Eddie watched Elvis soar, he watched him bring rock'n'roll into every home in America and leave a changed culture in his slipstream. When The Cochran Brothers met him, at WMPS Radio in Memphis, Elvis was there for much the same reason as them, for gladhanding and promotion and charming DJs into spinning records. The meeting between Eddie and Elvis was hurried, little more than a hi and a handshake between two young men who were about to help change the world.

Red Matthews's management approach wasn't working out brilliantly. His main contribution to The Cochran Brothers seems to have been quoting exaggerated sales figures to the music press and encouraging them to play and practice together in the hopes of becoming big country stars. Red, like many, had not yet realised that a tide was turning. Money was low by the time Eddie and Hank shook Elvis Presley's hand in Memphis and Red decided it would be a good time to cut out and head off, leaving Eddie and Hank stranded and a long way from Bell Gardens. Guitars in hand, having sold Eddie's amp for money for supplies, they started the long hitch-hike back to California, picking up a few dollars playing where they could and sleeping in a chicken coop. Bell Gardens was waiting for them when they got home, as, of course, was the Bell Gardens Music Centre.

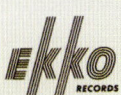

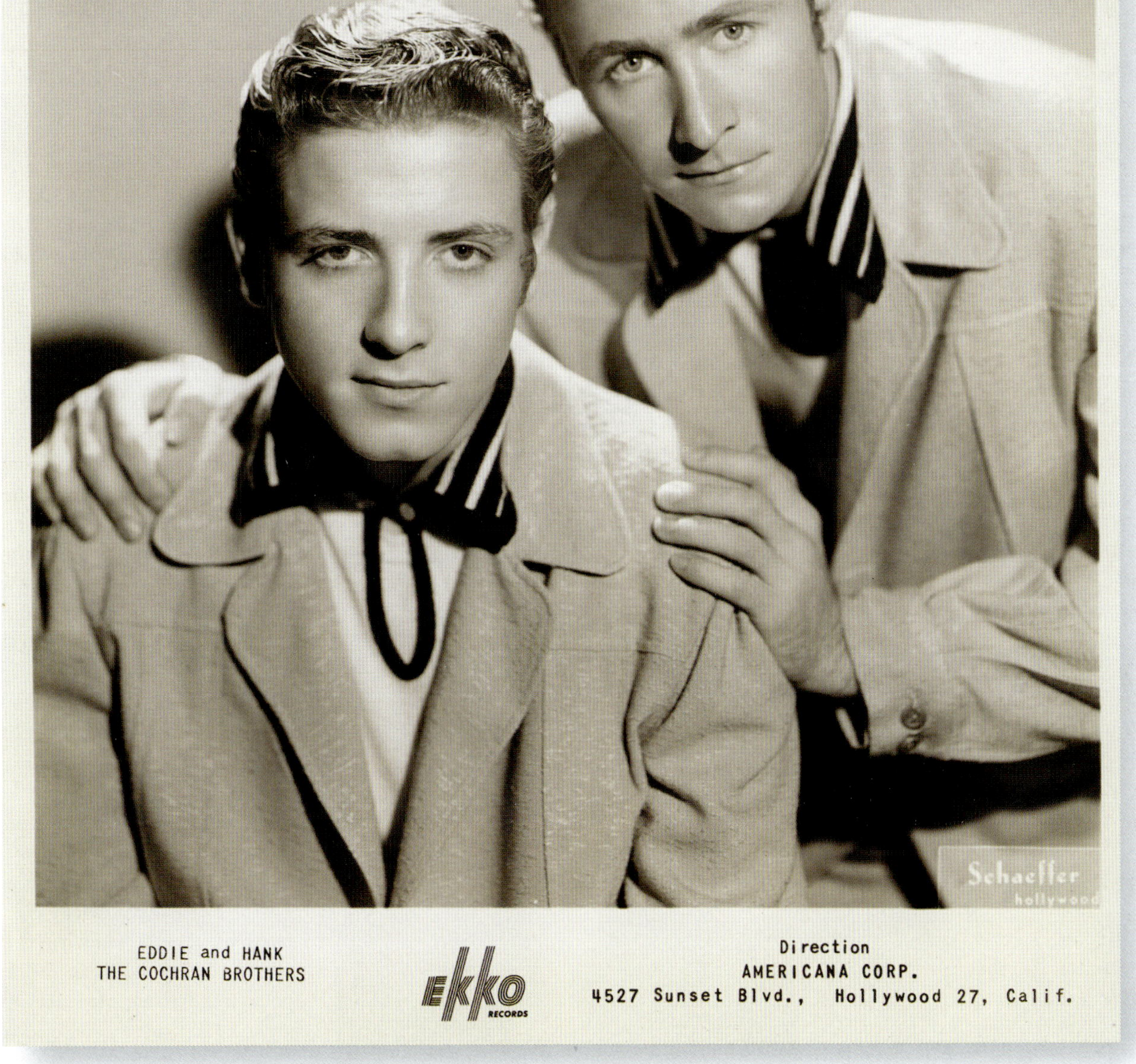
Schaeffer
hollywood
EDDIE and HANK
THE COCHRAN BROTHERS
EKKO
RECORDS
Direction
AMERICANA CORP.
4527 Sunset Blvd., Hollywood 27, Calif.

Chapter Four

IF YOU HUNG around the Music Centre long enough then chances are you'd bump into Jerry Capehart. Jerry was doing pretty good for himself, he knew what he wanted and had his eyes on the prize. Every Sunday night he could be found at The Squeakin' Deacon Show, a local radio show broadcast on KXLA and presented by Carl 'Deacon' Moore which was popular with musicians from the area who liked to hang out there. Jerry was a Korean War veteran and a talented songwriter with a track record. His song, 'Beautiful Brown Eyes', had been a chart hit for Rosemary Clooney and Jimmy Wakely, and Jerry had liked how having a hit felt. He had a bunch more songs, a bunch more potential hits, all he needed was the right way to present them.

Eddie and Jerry were introduced by the owner of Bell Gardens Music Centre and Jerry Capehart thought he'd landed upon the ideal way to showcase his songs in the form of The Cochran Brothers. Soon, Eddie, Hank and Jerry were working together in the tiny studio out back of the Music Centre where they recorded Jerry's songs direct to disc, which produced an acetate, a fragile record whose quality would worsen every time it was played. Although recording direct to disc may have saved on costly studio time and achieved Jerry's aim of having versions of his songs that he could play to people, the acetate disc itself was very delicate and prone to deterioration, meaning that most of the material recorded in those sessions, bar three songs, turned to dust and was lost forever. As well as employing The Cochran Brothers in the studio, where he was keeping rhythm by banging on whatever box was around, Jerry also began using them as his backing band when he played live. Jerry's increasing interest in The Cochran Brothers was the final straw for erstwhile manager Red Matthews, who chose this moment to bow out of the Eddie Cochran story.

Aside from working with Jerry, The Cochran Brothers remained a popular live draw and were racking up yet more exposure on local radio and TV shows. At one gig, Eddie was nowhere to be seen as the announcer started to introduce The Cochran Brothers. Hank made his way to a hidden area behind the stage where Eddie was deep in a philosophical discussion with a local girl. Hank called a halt to proceedings, Eddie zipped up and grabbed his Gretsch and headed to the stage. It wasn't until after the show that Hank, exasperated at his partner's actions, told Eddie he needed to think with his brain a little more and his teenage libido a little less. When the pair drove down into Hollywood to visit Country legend Lefty Frizzell they blew a tyre en route. It was a bitterly cold night so the pair fixed the busted tyre as quickly as they could and went off to meet Lefty. The night got colder as they hung out in the studio, so when another tyre blew out on the way home they called brother Bob to come get them and left the motor running in the car to keep warm. By the time brother Bob arrived, Eddie and Hank had passed out from inhaling exhaust fumes and both had to be revived.

The two Cochran Brothers singles had flopped partly because the country market was pretty swamped already and partly because Ekko Records' promotion of the record wasn't what it might have been. But audiences kept showing up to see the band, so they kept on playing. By November 1955, Capehart was essentially managing The Cochran Brothers and had made a deal with a no-nonsense R'n'B loving, record store owning character from Watts in LA called John Dolphin. Dolphin had a recording studio set up out back of his record store where he could record straight to acetate, a process that Eddie, Jerry and Hank were already familiar with. Having a record store meant that as soon as the acetate was pressed, the in-house dee-jay, Huggy Boy, could play the song from the store's radio booth and provide John Dolphin with instant feedback as to whether there was an audience for a particular tune and whether or not he should press up a run of copies and sell them through his store. If he did decide to push forward with the release he had two record labels to choose from, Cash Records and Money Records, on which to put the tune out. The kind of country that The

(Above) Eddie and Jerry Capehart at Gold Star Studios.

(Left) Eddie's brother, Bob

Cochran Brothers were playing wasn't to Dolphin's taste, but he knew quality when he heard it and soon Eddie, Jerry and Hank were working with his band out back of the record store.

The Cochran Brothers recorded a couple of Jerry's songs with Dolphin's band, 'Walkin' Stick Boogie' and 'Rollin''. Perhaps the most impressive thing about the recordings is Eddie's guitar parts. Although the context of the songs is trad country, in the lead guitar you can hear Eddie Cochran beginning to hone the sound that would soon become unmistakeable. The Cochran Brothers got a name-check on the label of Jerry's 45 when it was released in January of 1956 on Cash Records, along with a new name, J. Grey, who also appeared in connection with the song, credited as a composer. J. Grey was a pseudonym that John Dolphin used. Part of the one-single deal that Jerry made with Dolphin involved him taking credit on the song in lieu of payment for use of his studio and facilities.

All in all, it became apparent that neither Cash nor Money Records, specialising as they both did in R'n'B, were the right home for The Cochran Brothers and that one single was enough. Music was still divided in 1955; there were lines it didn't cross yet, there was still black music and white music and labels were still treating the two markets as separate. That would all change of course and the seeds of that change are visible in deals such as the one that Jerry and John Dolphin made. What came of the deal may not have been a roaring commercial success but what it symbolises is important, hillbilly music meeting R'n'B, a single example of the cross-fertilisation of cultures that was happening in real time in back room studios all over America. Eddie's trip to Dolphin's studio, his exposure to the side of the business serving the R'n'B market, cemented his love of the genre. R'n'B was dirty and tough and it had that howl n' growl that he dug so much.

Tweed sports coat and slicked back hair: an early Eddie promo shot.

Chapter Five

EDDIE WAS STARTING to cut loose on some of The Cochran Brothers' recordings, he was starting to find his sound. 'I'm Ready' sounds like rockabilly with a country twang. 'Tired and Sleepy' gives Eddie some room to add a vocal that hints of songs to come. The Cochran Brothers' reputation as a solid live act secured them gigs from California to Oregon and in the first months of 1956 they became regulars on the TV show *California Hayride*. The show was recorded close to San Francisco, so Eddie and Hank based themselves there for a while. The gigs and appearances kept coming. They played a residency with Jess Willard at the Napa Dream Bowl in Vallejo, performed at Jack and Chuck Wayne's club The Garden of Allah and appeared on the Hollywood Jubilee, a one-off gig on 10 March held at the El Monte Stadium. Eddie was young, he was learning every day and having fun and doing what he loved; he was living the dream before it was even a dream.

Although the long, long fuse that set it all off had been burning for a while, 1956 was the year that it all exploded, It had snaked its way through Legion halls, church halls, shotgun shacks and studios all over the country, where the music of America had merged and jumbled and styles had coalesced and reformed. R'n'B, country, street corner doo-wop and mountain songs had come together and a new music, a new art form, built out of society, technology and opportunity was born. They called it rock'n'roll, itself a slang reference for getting laid, and it became unstoppable. The roots of rock'n'roll were mostly found in peasant music, story songs and invocations played on whatever was to hand in a manner intended to lift spirits or banish woes. It came from good time party music and broken-hearted, beat-down blues, it came from small towns and big cities, mountain tops and valley floors. Jazz was in the air too of course, creating new shapes, exploring new possibilities and reminding those listening that rules can bend and break. The new sound was a revelation, a revolution. This new sound, made from all of these old sounds, was expressing more than religious fervour or mawkish sentiment, it was beginning to trade in flaming desire, fast cars and heartbreak, and it was beginning to shake its hips.

To some, already hopped up on the commie threat and bible study, rock'n'roll was anathema. It was all of their worst fears playing at 45rpm. These kids were rousing the devil and, just like the scriptures promised, the devil would want to come and play. Amongst the hype and the headlines there was some genuine moral outrage. To some, rock'n'roll seemed too unbridled, unpredictable and untameable, which was of course, why the kids dug it so much. The media amplified, sensationalised and exaggerated the anti-rock'n'roll voices by giving them a platform and made sure that rockin' was far from plain sailing at first. Rock'n'roll scared some people and offended others. It was the beginning of the end, a thousand nights in Sodom, the glorification of the carnal and a direct line to the devil, who was obviously the show-runner in chief and grabbing the best tunes for himself. Shaky black and white footage still survives of Reverend Jimmie Rodgers Snow, a southern pastor, preaching to his flock on the evils of rock'n'roll, summing up those deep dark fears and sending his congregation away convinced of the power of the new music to light fires that were impossible to put out. The Reverend Snow knew what he was talking about, his father was country legend, Hank Snow. He'd spent some time singing the Devil's music himself and toured with Elvis before seeing the light and finding God.

"I know how it feels when you sing it, I know what it does to you and I know the evil feeling that you feel when you sing it. I know the lost position that you get into in the beat. If you talk to the average teenager of today and you ask them what it is about rock'n'roll that they like, the first thing they'll say is the beat, the beat, the beat."

The established media, as always ready to stoke panic and fuel outrage, perhaps didn't even realise at first that the more they wrote about rock'n'roll, the more records they sold. Rock'n'roll began to get its own dedicated publications, teen magazines appeared on the shelves filled with interviews with the new stars. The magazines featured pictures of those stars relaxing or at work, gossip about who was dating who, short articles and softly lit close-up swoon shots for you to pull out and pin on to your wall. Ever keen to turn a buck, it didn't take record companies and the wider showbiz industry long to recognise that there was a whole new audience out there and serving them could be very profitable indeed. This new demographic, the much touted 'teenager', had time to kill and money to spend, they wanted something that was theirs, something that spoke to them, something by them and for them. Rock'n'roll and its roots was the unifier they were looking for, it dug into the universal, it was their own reflection. For a short, beautiful moment, it was perfect.

The widening schism which would come to be known as the generation gap had cracked open, as far as rock'n'roll was concerned, the previous year. Hollywood rolled the dice early on and gambled that movies aimed at teenagers, films that reflected their experience back to them, had a decent chance of scoring big at the box office. They were right. *Blackboard Jungle* was released in 1955 and immediately captured the imagination of the new audience while it thrilled and scandalised their parents. The movie, based on a novel by Evan Hunter and directed by Richard Brooks, was the first to use rock'n'roll in its soundtrack and begins with Bill Haley's 'Rock Around the Clock' blasting over the opening credits, the loudest that most of the kids in the theatres had ever heard rock'n'roll. The tinny radio sound and muted jukeboxes the audience were used to was replaced by an all-out sonic attack that sounded like a call to arms. They were blown out of their seats and onto their feet by the power and audacity of what they were hearing and how loud they were hearing it, and cinemas up and down America suddenly became impromptu dancehalls. Once the credits rolled, the film's plot dealt with race, juvenile delinquency, anti-social behaviour and teenage angst and featured an unforgettable breakout performance from Sidney Poitier. The movie was high melodrama, juvenile delinquents with switchblade knives, hip talk, hep talk and explosive teen tempers. The new audience, the teenagers, loved it. It spoke their language and showed them a raw and uncompromising version of their own story, for most of them, an extreme example. *Blackboard Jungle* got outright banned in some places, the Atlanta Citizen Review Board called it 'immoral', 'obscene', and 'licentious', while in other towns they turned the volume down to zero at the start of the movie while the evil Bill Haley and his devilish Comets tempted the kids with decadence and sin. Bill Haley had played an important role in warming the world up to rock'n'roll. His 'Rock Around the Clock' went to number one for eight weeks and the new movement was off to the races.

Seventeen-year-old Eddie Cochran's 1956 began much as his 1955 had ended. He'd gone from pulling brother Bill's old Kay guitar from the cupboard at home to stepping up on stage

with a brand new 6120 and leaving to hollering and applause, he'd gone from studio novice to experimenter with sound, he'd gone from practising alone to being able to jam with whoever was around, no matter that he was still always the youngest guy in the room. Eddie was growing up live on stage, he knew his purpose and he was having the time of his life heeding its call. Eddie was becoming ambitious. He was also beginning to get more interested in what most young men his age are interested in, namely getting drunk now and then, and chasing after the girls who were starting to be everywhere he looked. Where girls were concerned, Eddie didn't have to try too hard. His good looks coupled with his effortless style and growing local celebrity status ensured that he found a place in the hearts of many of the females who seemed to be around more and more. Eddie was from a big family and used to being around people, he was good fun and able to hold his own in whichever company he found himself, be it amongst older, more experienced musicians or the gaggle of female fans who were beginning to gather at his feet during shows or wait for him at the end of his performance. Eddie liked people, people liked Eddie. He continued to take any chance he could to play, record or write music. It was all he did now.

Eddie returned to John Dolphin's studio in February of 1956 along with Jerry and a band that featured a guitar idol of Eddie's, Joe Maphis. They got 'Rockin' and Flyin'' down at the session with Jerry singing, the instrumental backing track of which was released as 'Fast Jivin'' on Hollywood Records and credited to Ernie 'Jivin' Around' Freeman. Tellingly, there is no sign of Hank Cochran being involved in the session, indicative perhaps of the rift growing between Eddie and Jerry on the one hand, and Hank on the other. The songs recorded during the session once again highlight the evolution of Eddie Cochran as a guitar player as his style was becoming more unique and recognisable. Eddie and Hank continued to work together though and provided backing band services for Cash Records on the Don Deal songs, 'Cryin' In One Eye' and 'Broken Hearted Fellow', as well as continuing to work on Jerry's material. So busy was Eddie during this period that compiling a list of what he played on and when is a nigh-on impossible task. If you didn't need a guitar player, Eddie might come along and add drums or piano or help you overdub for a fuller, richer sound. The sessions where he played guitar though, show the Eddie Cochran sound emerging. The 6120 was starting to let him pick and twang like Chet and growl like the blues guys and it was starting to let him sound like Eddie Cochran.

(Opposite) The Country & Western Caravan On Tour. The three headliners were Eddie, Johnny Horton and Marvin Rainwater.

(Top) Eddie and Earl McDaniel, one of LA's most popular DJs in the late fifties, at Gold Star.

(Bottom) Everything Eddie did, he did with a sense of humour.

Chapter Six

GOLD STAR STUDIOS was in Hollywood, at the corner of Santa Monica and Vine, and had earned the reputation as the place to go if you wanted to record a decent demo but didn't want to pay high-end studio prices. The studio had been opened in 1950 by Stan Ross and Dave Gold who, instead of buying in equipment to kit it out, had often just built their own. The business grew and they added another studio to the operation in 1956. As when they'd set up Gold Star six years previous, much of the new studio was equipped with Dave's hand-built consoles. There was a good sound in the room, it added its own magical space and reverb for bands like The Champs, who recorded the party anthem 'Tequila' there, and would go on to cement its reputation some years later when Phil Spector used it as a site to perfect his Wall of Sound and Steven Stills recorded there with Buffalo Springfield.

Eddie Cochran and Jerry Capehart started attending the twenty-five dollar an hour Gold Star Studio B for ten-hour Wednesday sessions. The sessions were hosted by American Music. American Music was filled with musicians and Wednesdays at Gold Star soon became everyone's favourite day of the week. They would jam with whoever was around, Dave Fitzsimmons might play piano and bassman Guybo was, of course, a regular. Eddie and Guybo had played together for so long now that that they could read each other's moves and chase down structures and grooves together as Jerry beat out his rhythms on a cardboard box. The sessions gave Eddie more time to indulge his passion for the possibilities of sound. Studio B was the cheaper of the two studios, nonetheless, Eddie and Jerry pushed it to the edge of its capabilities and produced music there that, to their ears, sounded as good as anything on the *Billboard* top 10. Eddie worked best when he had people to bounce off, when he was in an environment where he could both shine and learn. The more he played and recorded with other people, the better he became.

In April of 1956, a session at Gold Star produced the first version of the classic, 'Pink Peg Slacks'. The song chimed perfectly with the times. As well as their unrelenting love of music, the new teenage audience were also becoming very interested in fashion, in how what they wore sent a message out into the world about who they were. To previous generations, clothes had been seen on the whole as utilitarian and functional, whereas now they were starting to be viewed more and more as a means of expression. Clothes started to become signifiers of wider interests, they started to become the way that the tribes forming within the new youth culture could recognise each other. A black leather motorcycle jacket sent one message, a college letterman jacket another. 'Pink Peg Slacks' rocked along telling the story of a young man, who, whilst out at night seeing a show is confronted with a pair of rayon acetate high waisted pink pants in a department store window. The pants become a twelve-dollar obsession, but even with the sawbuck donated by his girlfriend's daddy, the cat is still two bucks short. His burning, insatiable desire to own those crazy pants remains undiminished throughout the song despite all of the setbacks he encounters on his journey. The song's writing is credited to Jerry Capehart and The Cochran Brothers, it's cool and loose and there's an insistent groove to it. What's most notable about the recording of 'Pink Peg Slacks' though, and the reason the song is so convincing, is that it's Eddie Cochran singing it. Eddie sang three songs that day. No one there at the time realised what had happened, not really. Jerry didn't realise, Guybo didn't realise, Hank didn't realise and Eddie didn't either. No-one realised the potency and potential of Eddie Cochran singing a song that spoke directly to the new audience in their own language. No-one realised that they'd hit the jackpot, that they'd aligned all the necessary elements and arranged the formula and now that Eddie was up front and they were starting to rock, they'd hit upon solid gold.

Rock'n'roll was fast becoming a representation of what was going on in the country. It quickly developed its own language and style and spread through first America, then the world. The audience was beginning to realise that it had power, it was seeing itself as separate and autonomous. In the context of The Cochran Brothers, Eddie was all in on the new music, Hank not so much and something had to give. Hank and Eddie were pulling in different directions. In the spring of '56 they recorded together at a session to get four songs down that they'd written with Jerry. They found themselves back in Hollywood, at Western Recorders, but this time they eschewed the trappings of the western swing The Cochran Brothers had been trading in and instead let rip and went pure, full-on rockabilly. The songs they got down during that session were 'Tired and Sleepy', 'Fool's Paradise', 'Open the Door' and 'Slow Down'. Ekko Records were still on board and two songs recorded at the session, 'Tired and Sleepy' and 'Fool's Paradise' were released as a single which, like the previous two Cochran Brothers songs, didn't really do any business. Though they didn't know it at the time, the Western Recorders session would mark the last time that The Cochran Brothers would officially record together.

(Above) Pushing boundaries and honing his craft. Eddie in the studio.

(Right) One more take. Eddie and Jerry searching for their sound.

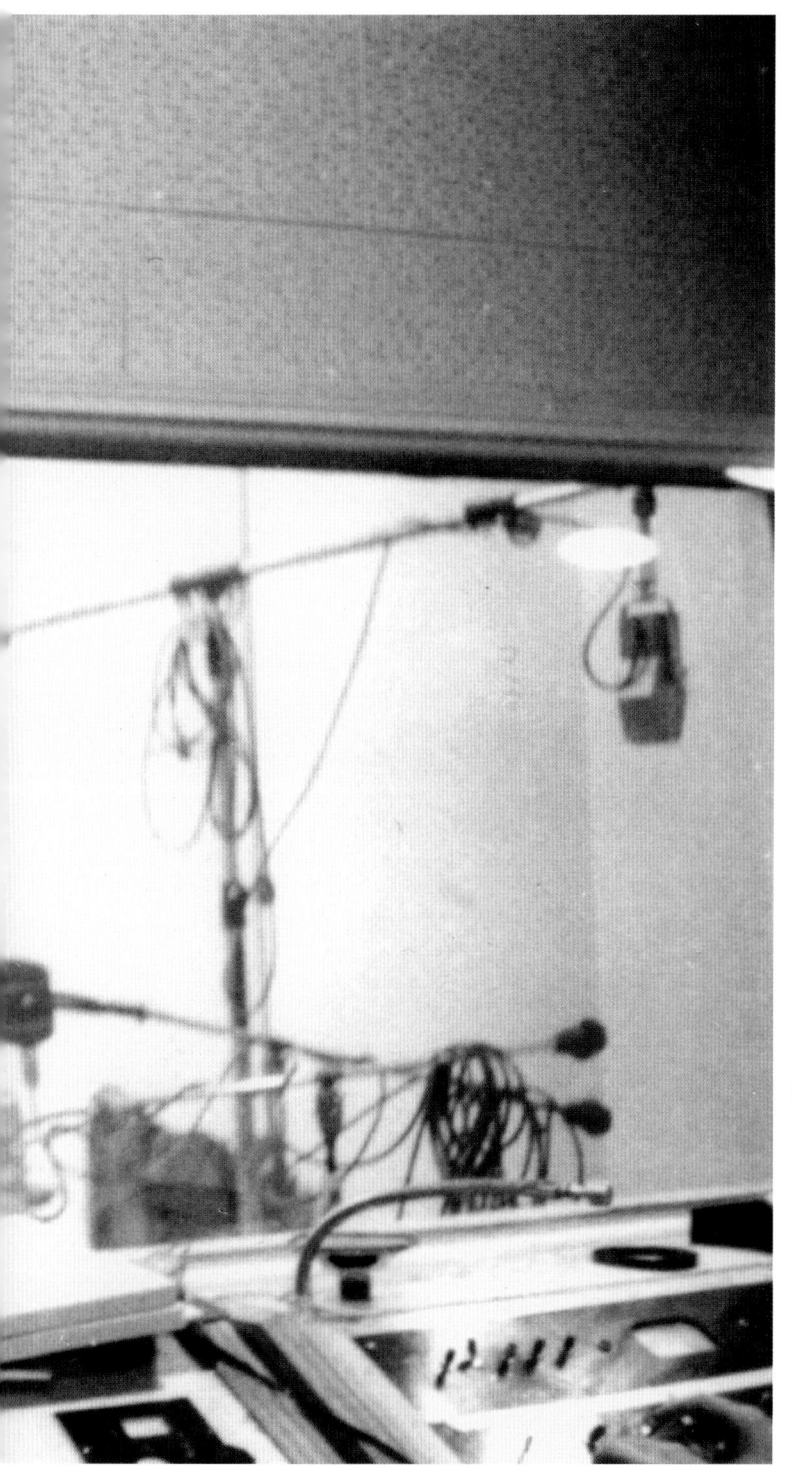

One immediate consequence of Eddie stepping forward was that Hank Cochran would have to take a step back. The Cochran Brothers had been an important step on both and Hank and Eddie's musical journeys but the times they were a-changing. Hank's heart was pure country, he was a rhinestone suit, honky-tonk guy to his core. Rock'n'roll was too hysterical for Hank, the fans were too crazy and the gigs were too wild. Plus, Hank wasn't convinced about Jerry, he didn't like that he claimed credit for songs he didn't write and he wasn't down with the way Jerry operated. Hank Cochran, even as a teenager, was old school. He was married with a kid already and looking to move out to San Francisco to take up a regular spot on the California Hayride. Eddie Cochran was a new breed, he was all of his favourite genres at once. His journey to rock'n'roll via country music and western swing was echoed in the story of Buddy Holly down in Lubbock, Texas, other people were making their way to it via gospel or the blues, but however they were getting there, once they hit upon rock'n'roll, they were making it their own.

Hank didn't fade off into the background once The Cochran Brothers finally disbanded in June 1956 over their growing musical differences. His background was tough and chaotic, he was used to a little challenge and adversity, it's what gave him the drive to keep hitchhiking toward his dream. Hank stayed country and proved he was a songwriting force to be reckoned with when he penned a bunch of hits after splitting with Eddie, including Patsy Cline's late-nite heartbreak classic, 'I Fall to Pieces'. Hank Cochran did well, he got married five times and made it all the way to the Country Music Hall of Fame.

Chapter Seven

THE SESSION WORK was rolling in for Eddie. His adaptability played in his favour, the way he could switch from trad country to rockabilly and all stations between meant that no matter what the session, Eddie could contribute. He kept his ego in check despite his stature and growing reputation, he was still humble and fun to be around and most importantly, still eager to learn. He continued working his musical muscles with the session work and the Wednesday American Music shindigs at Gold Star. He began to work on his voice there now, too. Having heard himself on songs such as 'Pink Peg Slacks', Eddie could see where his strengths were as a vocalist, where his weaknesses were and what worked and what didn't. As for fixing what didn't, Eddie did what he always did where music was concerned, he practised every chance he got and, by virtue of his solid gold ear and his dedication, he perfected it. Eddie's singing style started to become an avenue for his sense of humour and his sincerity, and he started to enjoy it. The more he enjoyed it the looser he got and the looser he got, the better he sounded. Freed of the country constraints of The Cochran Brothers, Eddie continued to indulge his wild side and recorded a couple of what would later be considered rock'n'roll classics from the early canon.

In June of '56 he laid down versions of 'Long Tall Sally' and 'Blue Suede Shoes' with Guybo on bass and Jerry's trademark cardboard box drums keeping rhythm. 'Long Tall Sally' was Little Richard's number one smash, backed by the equally stellar 'Slippin' and Slidin'' and had been released as the follow-up to 'Tutti Frutti'. 'Tutti Frutti' did good business and introduced the world to Richard Wayne Penniman who, despite seemingly exploding onto the culture from nowhere, had been steadily putting out records since 1951. Little Richard had gospel and the blues running through him like electricity, he levitated at the piano keys looking male and female and good and bad and he shone like he was lit from within. In another in a series of watershed moments in rock'n'roll that were coming thick and fast in 1956, 'Tutti Frutti' sold a million copies. Pat Boone, a staid crooner who typified everything that rock'n'roll wasn't, released a cover of the song that got to number twelve in the charts, even higher than Little Richard's original. Boone's cover of Little Richard's tune highlights again the divided nature of music in 1956. Little Richard saw what was happening and remarked many years later that although the white kids may have had Pat Boone on their dresser, they'd have 'me in the drawer 'cause they like my version better.'

They'd have been right to. From its opening refrain to its cleaned-up but still kinda filthy lyrics, the song is a perfect work of rock'n'roll art. Eddie's recording of such tunes put him squarely at the heart of the new culture. In making them, he had arrived at exactly where he needed to be. Eddie Cochran wasn't quite among the first wave of rock'n'rollers, but he wasn't far behind.

While Eddie was refining his stage and studio skills, Elvis Presley released his debut RCA single, 'Heartbreak Hotel', and the whole world changed. The song, based on the newspaper story of a suicide who'd ended it all by jumping from a hotel window, spent seven weeks on top of the Billboard chart, and suddenly Elvis was everywhere.

Elvis Presley had been in and out of Sun Records since 1953 when he'd recorded his first demo there. Sun was owned by Sam Phillips, a vital early advocate and provider of rockabilly, hillbilly, jump-blues, R'n'B, gospel and early rock'n'roll to the masses. The fire burned deep in Sam. As a child he was obsessed by radio, it took the young Sam Phillips away somewhere, it fired his imagination and let his very singular mind travel where it would. When that same young Sam then found himself up to his neck in the blues, experiencing a sonic epiphany on Beale Street in Memphis at five o'clock in the morning, the die was cast. That moment in New Orleans spoke to Sam and stayed with him forever, it got into his bones and he was sold. Back then every corner of Beale Street was music, if they didn't have instruments they sang acapella and stomped their feet to keep time. Sam Phillips bought that feeling to the world and span it into gold. He gambled early on that if he could find a white boy with a black sound and a black feel then the music he loved would reach white America, and they would love it too. He'd seen first-hand the segregation of musical genres and the wider segregation of the southern US and saw that through music he had an opportunity to start working on breaking those divisions down a little, and if he could make a few bucks while he did it, then all the better. Phillips knew deep down in his soul that what was called black music was in fact, music for everybody, same for white music. Sam knew that if a tune is going to fire you up or break your heart it isn't going to care about what colour you are. He knew that a rockin' tune is a rockin' tune, no matter who's playing it. His gamble was that other people would know it too. Sam's credentials where rock'n'roll was concerned were bona-fide, he was producing rock'n'roll records before they even had a name. 'Rocket 88' by Jackie Brenston and his Delta Cats, the nom-de-plume of Ike Turner and his Kings of Rhythm, is a Sam Phillips production recorded five years before Elvis sang about a Heartbreak Hotel,

The acetate for the 'Pink Peg Slacks' demo, recorded for American Music Inc in April 1956 at Eddie's very first Gold Star Studios session. It marked the first time that Eddie had taken the mic for lead vocals.

and is often cited as the tune that most defined the shape of things to come.

'That's All Right', Elvis's first single for Sun Records and released in '54 was pure reverb drenched southern rockabilly. In 1954, rockabilly was one point where styles, influences and attitudes were crashing into one another and creating something new. Rockabilly mixed bluegrass, country, jump blues, boogie-woogie and western swing and when you heard it, you wanted to shake, drink, fight and fuck. Rockabilly pointed in the direction that rock'n'roll was headed, though at first the term was just as likely to be used as an insult. The rockabilly sound was excitement, strong liquor, sex and good times, all stripped back and played fast, wild and loud. It was infectious and soul-stirring and in the mid-fifties, Elvis Presley, Johnny Cash and Carl Perkins were recording it for posterity over at Sun Studios in Memphis. Eddie Cochran had rockabilly down. Its influences were his influences and he spoke its language, he had done for a while. The Cochran Brothers rendition of 'I'm Ready', recorded with Jerry playing box drums and Hank singing, featured a glorious rockabilly guitar part from Eddie that turned a pretty good song into a killer.

Sam Phillips made his living searching out the underground, finding some of the most iconic figures in rock'n'roll history and sharing his discoveries with the world. One legendary Sun Records jam session, in December of 1956, began as a Carl Perkins session, with Jerry Lee Lewis playing piano. Though he'd left the label the previous year, Elvis showed up and joined them so Sam called in Johnny Cash and the four hung out and sang and played a while. Carl Perkins was a big star by the time he sat around the piano with Jerry Lee, Johnny and Elvis. His version of 'Blue Suede Shoes', released in January of 1956, had been a smash, at one point selling twenty thousand copies a day. But Carl was lucky to be there. In March of 1956 he'd been en route with his band to inject a little real life rock'n'roll into Perry Como's TV show when the car they were in was involved in a crash so serious that it was written off. Sam Phillips bought Carl a brand new Cadillac to replace his wreck, which Carl then proceeded to write off in another smash. The pictures of Carl, Jerry Lee, Johnny and Elvis at Sun bear testament to Sam Phillips' genius, to his ability to spot talent and his huge and undeniable influence on early rock'n'roll. When the Memphis Press Scimitar published the photographs the next day the term 'Million Dollar Quartet' was used to describe the four travellers in song, and it stuck.

Elvis Presley had started to get big while he was with Sun Records, real big. So big that the established entertainment industry, in the form of RCA Victor, came knocking and announced that they were interested in buying Presley's contract, moving him away from the limited resources available to him at Sun and putting the weight of the RCA corporate machine behind him. Sam was amused, he threw them an astronomical, impossible figure, he said he wanted $35,000 for Presley's contract. He said that if they paid him that, then the kid from Tupelo Mississippi was all theirs. To the surprise of Sam Phillips and many others, RCA Victor didn't flinch, and wrote the cheque.

The money that Phillips took for Elvis's contract seems a paltry sum now, but the $35,000 RCA paid Phillips for Elvis was a huge amount of money to Sam back then. Sun Records was an independent record label and a fat bank roll in Sam's pocket enabled him to combat the cash flow problems that plagued labels like his up and down the country.

Ray Stanley and Dale Fitzsimmons, senior staff over at American Music Publishing, listened to 'Pink Peg Slacks' and the other four songs recorded at Gold Star and liked what they heard, and in Eddie, they liked what they saw. He was almost tailor-made for the times. Aside from his obvious feel for the new music he was cool enough that the guys would want to hang with him and that twinkle in his eye and his boyish good looks ensured the girls would dig him too. Eddie's natural ability and affinity with rock'n'roll played in his favour. A deal was done and Crest Records, a subsidiary of American Music, got ready to release Eddie Cochran's first single, 'Skinny Jim', in July. The song was a rockin' Cochran and Capehart composition telling the story of a guy without an ounce of fat on him who steals Eddie's girl away from him at a party. They'd recorded the song at Master Recorders Studio on 533 North Fairfax Avenue. Jerry Capehart had high hopes for the song and saw it as the chance he'd been looking for, an opportunity to open some doors, to grease some wheels. Armed with 'Skinny Jim' and three more tracks, Jerry went out to find them a deal.

Chapter Eight

EARLY ROCK'N'ROLL had gathered an array of performers, each with their own unique identity and approach. Eddie didn't come across as gloriously high on the new religion as Little Richard or as down-home possessed and demonic as Jerry Lee Lewis would, but he was a believer. Always eager to be polite to whoever was introducing or interviewing him but keen to get past them and play new music to this new audience, to connect and feel it with them. Eddie was still more day to day than Elvis, who was already amassing a driveway full of the cars that Eddie dreamed of owning. Presley was peacock proud and built out of rim shot rhythm and had already been anointed the Godhead of rock'n'roll. Elvis was showing people like Eddie that if they got it right, the sky was the limit. Whatever 'it' was, for a while, Elvis was it. While Jerry was out shopping for a deal, Eddie was working hard, taking every job he could get and devoting himself to music 24/7, but he was getting lucky. The next big opportunity 1956 had in store for him was an appearance in the movie, *The Girl Can't Help It*. There are conflicting stories of how Eddie got the part, though it looks to have been through a chance meeting with director Boris Petroff who just so happened to have a friend who was looking for rock'n'rollers to perform in his new Jayne Mansfield movie. The film was scheduled to start shooting as soon as Jayne completed her run on Broadway in the play *Will Success Spoil Rock Hunter?*. *The Girl Can't Help It*, originally titled *Do-Re-Mi* lined up an impressive musical cast, Little Richard was in the movie, so was Fats Domino and a figure who would go on to figure heavily in Eddie's life and legacy, Gene Vincent.

Liberty Records had been around since Simon Waronker set it up in 1955. Julie London, the de facto musical star of *The Girl Can't Help It*, was signed to the label where she scored a huge hit with her torch-song classic, 'Cry Me A River'. In 1959, when the payola scandal hit the music business, Liberty was one of the only record companies found not to be taking part in the practice. Payola was, essentially, a bribe paid in order to get a particular song or artist played on the air. It meant, potentially, that bad records could crowd out good by virtue of their record company's deep pockets. By the mid-fifties, payola was almost an established method of record promotion. Thousands of dollars could change hands with no record of the transaction and suddenly, someone had a hit. As well as airplay on radio, inclusion on jukeboxes was highly prized and secured by bribes. Hi-Fidelity jukeboxes had played their part pre-rock'n'roll from the 1940s by spreading the gospel of doo-wop. The first jukebox machine engineered to play 45rpm records was built in 1950. Jukeboxes gave record companies the opportunity to get their product to market and see how it fared against the competition and were ripe for exploitation. Jukeboxes were try-before-you-buy advertising for artists and labels. They were also, crucially, a point where black music could meet a receptive white audience.

To hear Si Waronker tell it, a 17-year-old Eddie Cochran secured his deal with Liberty Records by turning up at the label day after day and sitting there until, four days in, Si had to agree to listen to the kid who was sitting in reception. Si liked what he heard and was immediately convinced that this Eddie Cochran kid had something. To hear Jerry Capehart tell it, it was he, rather than Eddie who spent day after day at Liberty in his new role as manager until he got his chance to present the label with Eddie's demos. So taken were Liberty that they told Jerry they'd sign Eddie immediately. Jerry made a beeline for Priory Street where he outlined the offer to Eddie and Alice. The matter was discussed over a family dinner and Eddie met the Liberty executives the following morning when he went over to talk through the fine print on his contract and meet Si face to face. However it happened, in Liberty Records Eddie had found a musical home, a much-needed record deal and an enthusiastic and sympathetic label boss. Si Waronker had music in him, he'd been a violin prodigy as a child and played on film scores over at Twentieth Century Fox. Waronker had fight in him too, as a child he'd fled from Nazi Germany. In the early days of Liberty, Si had wanted jazz singer Bobby Troup to sign to his fledgling label but Bobby was happy where he was. Bobby suggested instead that Si sign his girlfriend, Julie London. Si signed Julie to the label and released 'Cry Me A River', the song was a smash and Liberty Records was up and running. Eddie signed with the label on 8 September 1956. The contract secured him 5 per cent of every dollar his records earned, once he'd paid back the cost of recording them, and no sooner had the ink dried on it than tours were booked and Eddie was offered a part in another movie. This time he played a hep-talking, mumbling, juvenile delinquent named Bong in a film called *Untamed Youth*. With the Liberty deal secure, he set about recording as much material as he could. Songs that would go on to become classics were first sketched out in the Gold Star sessions that followed his signing to the label. Eddie continued to take session work wherever he could fit it in, and to get into the yuletide spirit to round out the year, Eddie and Guybo both played on Liberty's novelty yuletide release, The Holly Twins' 'I Want Elvis For Christmas'.

Hollywood calling. He may not have been a star yet, but he sure looked and sounded like one. Eddie in *The Girl Can't Help It*.

Chapter Nine

THE GIRL CAN'T *Help It* started life as a vehicle to introduce to one of Hollywood's hottest new Marilyn Monroe-inspired bombshells and would have been considered pretty standard mid-fifties Hollywood fare if it weren't for its inclusion of some of the coolest rockers in the country and the fact that it hit the screens just as the desire to see and hear those very same rockers was becoming insatiable. The film became an instant rock'n'roll classic. Though it had come to him from left-field, Eddie knew the opportunity to feature in the movie was a good one and that in order to do it justice, he needed the right song. He needed a tune that told the world who he was. After much deliberation It was decided that Eddie should perform 'Twenty Flight Rock' in the film, a song originally written by an American Music staff writer by the name of Nelda Fairchild, although when it finally appeared, it would be credited as a Fairchild/Cochran composition. 'Twenty Flight Rock' is a counting song, like Bill Haley's 'Rock Around the Clock'. In it, Eddie's girl lives uptown, way up on the twentieth floor, but the elevator is broken down in her building and away being repaired in Chicago. Eddie can't stay away but by the time he's climbed the stairs to his girl's place, he's too tired to rock. They recorded the song with Guybo playing the bull fiddle and Jerry keeping rhythm on an old soup box.

In the 1950s, cinemagoing was a very different experience to what it has become. Theatres offered a full programme of entertainment including cartoons, ads, a b-movie and the main feature. B-movies were often hastily and cheaply produced sensationalist affairs aimed at turning a quick buck by taking a hot topic, wrapping a quick script and a flimsy plot around it and putting it in front of the public as quickly as possible. *The Girl Can't Help It* had high production values and an expensive look and of all the films that included rock'n'roll, it was by far one of the best. The colour in the film is sumptuous, the set piece

musical numbers are cool too. Gene Vincent and his Blue Caps perform 'Be-Bop-a-Lula', Fats Domino sings 'Blue Monday' and Little Richard tears the screen up three different times. There was talk at one point of Elvis appearing in the movie but it became obvious early on that Colonel Tom Parker's price for his boy was going to be way too high. That worked out well for Eddie, Elvis's absence gave the stars that did appear in the movie the chance to shine, without being obscured by the sun. *The Girl Can't Help It* hit the cinemas at Christmastime 1956 and projected Eddie fifteen feet tall singing 'Twenty Flight Rock' to movie-goers all over the country. In the movie, Eddie is introduced as one of the hottest rockers around and plays his part perfectly. Eddie shot his appearance at the Fox studio on West Pico Boulevard and had obviously been directed to put as much Elvis into his performance as possible, but Eddie Cochran still shone through. Eddie's set piece in the movie is just him in his Cochran Brothers box jacket, striped shirt and loose pants framed by a theatrical curtain next to his Magnatone Maestro amp. With no band behind him and nothing to distract from his performance save the cutaway reaction shots to it, Eddie fills the screen with confidence and comes across like he belongs there. He looked good in the film, so cool, so confident, so right. Frame by frame, the Eddie Cochran silhouette was imprinted onto rock'n'roll in glorious technicolour. He was now the blond, good-looking kid with the Gretsch in the baggy pants playing perfect rock'n'roll. The new, looser cut clothes in lightweight rayons and gaberdines hung well on Eddie, they showed movement, they exaggerated it, he didn't have to do much to look like he was doing a lot. With *The Girl Can't Help It* beginning to play in theatres, Eddie was soon performing to thousands of cinemagoers every night and although he wasn't one quite yet, the movie made Eddie look, feel and sound like a star. Over in the UK, the film planted some very

A note from Eddie's pal, Johnnie Rook.

important seeds. In Liverpool, England, at a local fete where his band were performing, a young John Lennon met a kid called Paul McCartney who could only play 'Twenty Flight Rock', but also knew all of the words. Lennon was so knocked out by McCartney's impromptu performance of Eddie's tune that he asked him to join his band The Quarrymen. Paul said yes, and pretty soon the pair were writing songs together. Years later, when the Quarrymen had become The Beatles and conquered the world, they interrupted recording their *White Album* in order to head back to Paul's to watch *The Girl Can't Help It*'s British TV premiere.

As a result of his appearance in *The Girl Can't Help It*, Eddie met Johnny Rook, a would-be actor who'd been blown away upon first hearing 'Twenty Flight Rock', although he had assumed at first that the song was sung by one of the movie's other big stars, Gene Vincent. Johnny Rook fell into the film business following a chance encounter with movie-star Burt Lancaster who encouraged him to take the acting lessons over at the Pasadena Playhouse which led to Johnny landing his first roles. Johnny wanted to meet Eddie, and in order to get in touch, he left a note for him at the studio reception. The note was put with Eddie's growing bag of fan mail and correspondence where it stayed for a week until Alice found it, called Johnny and invited him over to Bell Gardens to meet her boy. Eddie was spending late nights in the studio, so Johnny headed over to Priory Street for eleven o'clock in the morning, allowing Eddie time to get up and get ready before his arrival. He needn't have worried about arriving on time. When he got to the Cochran house, Eddie was still crashed out in bed. Johnny filled the time waiting for the rocker to emerge by answering Alice's barrage of questions about where he was from, what food he liked to eat and what his star sign was. Eddie rose from his slumber and appeared in his bathrobe with messy hair and bleary eyes. He made his way to the stove and started to pour himself a coffee and hang a cigarette from his lip. Once his coffee was poured and his cigarette was lit, Eddie was able to face the world and meet

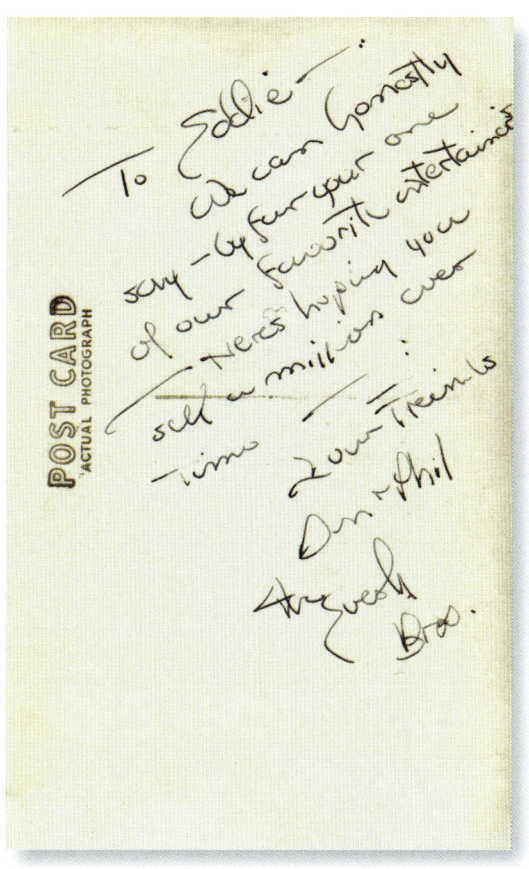

The Everly Brothers show Eddie some love.

his guest who, Alice was delighted to tell him, shared the same birth sign as Eddie and enjoyed cornbread and beans every bit as much as he did. Eddie and Johnny hung out in Eddie's room for a while listening to the recordings Eddie had made the previous day, Alice bought more coffee and Eddie did his Kingfish impression, got dressed and had Johnny head over to the Music Centre with him. Eddie needed guitar strings. Johnny noted how Eddie kind of had the run of the place at the Music Centre, how he could go in and pretty much help himself. Back at Priory Street, Johnny met Red, sister Gloria's husband, who was back from a day's work on his food truck. Red made no secret of the fact that he felt Jerry Capehart was holding Eddie back, that even with a star in the family times were still pretty tough and that given his position, Eddie should be able to contribute far more to the family's expenses. Red's take on Jerry wasn't unusual within Eddie's family, although at first at least, they hid the worst of their frustrations and suspicions of his manager from him. Alice must have taken to Johnny and invited him to stay to eat with them, so he and Eddie loaded up their plates and headed back to Eddie's room where he put on a Marty Robbins album for them to listen to as they ate.

The visit over, Eddie walked Johnny out to his car and the pair arranged to meet at the recording studio the next week. Johnny arrived at the studio and Eddie was there to meet him and introduce him to The Everly Brothers who'd just showed up too. They headed to the studio where Jerry was waiting and started work on a new number. Eddie was pulling on a whiskey bottle as he worked which contained his magical studio elixir, a mixture of honey and whiskey guaranteed to improve the voice and rejuvenate the spirits. Johnny offered to work for Eddie, to go out on the road promoting his records and raising his profile. Eddie liked the idea so off Johnny went. Upon his return a couple of weeks later, Johnny was privy to an argument between Eddie and Jerry, Eddie complaining that the material that was being selected for him was wrong and Jerry saying that he should record it anyway.

Hittin' the newsstands. Eddie graces the cover of *Dig* magazine, October 1957.

Chapter Ten

ROCK'N'ROLL WAS allowing those who made and performed it transcend the lives they had been born into and achieve something undreamt of. It was still as new to the artists as it was to the audience, they were all caught up in it together. This souped-up, syncopated blues bought optimism with it, it was an antidote to the economic trauma of their parents' generation and the pressure valve that the new audience so desperately needed. Kids from forgotten states were bringing their glorious noise to the masses, to their peers and their parents, and the masses were eating it up. The parents were still outraged, still looking into the void of the generation gap and seeing that they had lost control of their kids, or at least, that was the narrative still pursued by Hollywood and the tabloids. Jukeboxes, juke joints, hot-rods and loose women started regularly appearing in B-movies intended to thrill the drive-in kids and scare their parents silly.

Eddie's first single on Liberty was originally scheduled as 'Twenty Flight Rock'. It made sense, the song was a hit in *The Girl Can't Help It* and was, no matter how you looked at it, a stone cold rock'n'roll classic. Meanwhile though, Waronker had been eyeing up a John D. Loudermilk tune called 'Sittin' In The Balcony' for a while and was convinced that in the right hands it could be turned into a major hit. Waronker wanted to hedge his bets and maximise the return on his investment in Eddie and saw him as more than 'just' a rock'n'roll performer. As a result, Liberty Records changed their mind on Eddie's first single and instead of releasing 'Twenty Flight Rock' went for 'Sittin' In The Balcony' instead. Rock'n'roll was still too new, too much of an unknown quantity, it had only just been given a name and Waronker wanted to make sure that if it was a passing fad, Eddie wasn't tied directly to it, that he had a wider repertoire and an exit strategy. Waronker saw that Eddie's innate ability and the experience he was gaining working with musicians of all genres, from rockabilly to jazz, meant that he could turn his musical hand to pretty much anything and he saw Eddie as being able to cover all bases. After all, for all anyone knew, rock'n'roll might disappear as quickly as it had arrived and there'd be another craze along in a week. Waronker liked 'Sittin' In The Balcony' for Eddie and saw it as the perfect opportunity to widen his appeal. *The Girl Can't Help It* had established Eddie's rock'n'roll credentials, so the decision was taken to use the song to show another side of Eddie Cochran. The simple and irresistible 'Sittin' In The Balcony' was released in March 1957 and very quickly became a hit, spending thirteen weeks on the chart. For the flip side they selected 'Dark Lonely Street', a Cochran/Capehart composition. At first listen, 'Sittin' In The Balcony' is a little tame compared to 'Twenty Flight Rock', but listen closer and Eddie has injected some cartoon sleaze into the song with an overly lascivious vocal, and he's thrown in some country inflection and a comedy ending for good measure. Jerry Capehart described the song in an interview for the *History of Rock'n'Roll*.

"That was Eddie's first hit. Johnny Mann by the way did the arrangements on that with Eddie playing guitar, Connie Smith, Eddie's bass player Guybo who was also Eddie's best friend and myself playing on a cardboard box."

In order to capitalise on the success of the single, Eddie, with Guybo on bass and with Jerry Capehart now overseeing his career as full-blown manager, started touring. In April of 1957, at a gig in Philly at the Mastbaum Theatre, Eddie met Gene Vincent for the second time. The two were, by this point, crowned princes of rock'n'roll. They were tied by experiences that very few others shared, and they became friends immediately. Gene's original guitarist, Cliff Gallup, who'd helped define the Vincent sound on iconic recordings such as 'Be-Bop-a-Lula' and left the band the previous year, shared many of the same influences as Eddie, he dug Chet Atkins too and was, just like Eddie, formulating his own unique sound. Gene had started life as Vincent Eugene Craddock out of Norfolk Virginia and was a few years older than Eddie. When he'd dropped out of school and joined the Navy he was so young that his parents had had to sign his consent papers. Once enlisted, Gene spent time crewing at least three battleships and was, for a while, considering the Navy as

Eddie's the star, but Shrimper's the boss. Eddie, Shrimper and Patty.

a full blown career. In July of 1955, he was back in Norfolk and had just received over six hundred bucks from the Navy for re-enlisting. He used some of the cash to buy himself a Triumph motorcycle, the same Triumph motorcycle he was riding when a drunk driver smashed into him and did so much damage to his left leg that they thought at first that he might lose it. Gene didn't lose the leg, but the results of the motorcycle crash would stay with him forever. He limped from then on and managing the constant pain that he lived with became part of his daily routine. Gene's injury was wrapped in a cold steel sheath at Portsmouth Naval Hospital and he was discharged shortly after with a busted up leg, and his idea of staying in the Navy for the long haul gone forever. Once he was medically discharged from the military, Gene turned his attention to music, specifically rockabilly at first, and, backed by his band The Blue Caps (a slang term for sailors) he scored a big hit in 1956 with the classic 'Be-Bop-a-Lula' which spent twenty weeks on the Billboard Hot 100 and reached number seven. Gene hadn't written 'Be-Bop-a-Lula', his income never matched his fame but nonetheless, with 'Be-Bop-a-Lula', Gene Vincent carved his name into the history of rock'n'roll and ensured that no matter what happened, he would never die. Having such a big hit so early in his career though was a double-edged sword for Gene, it set the bar high and the fact that he could never again reach those dizzy heights of chart stardom played right into the hands of Gene Vincent's demons, of which there were many. On top of the painkillers he needed for his leg, Gene liked to drink. Problem was, Gene was a mean drunk, he became wild and mercurial, his mood would flip when he'd sunk a few and suddenly he'd become belligerent and aggressive. People make allowances for the bad behaviour of the famous or renowned, always have, always will, but Gene's behaviour was beginning to draw concerned glances. He found it harder and harder to repeat the chart success of 'Be-Bop-a-Lula' and started taking out the frustrations his lack of follow-up success bought on the world and whoever happened to be in the firing line, cementing his reputation of being difficult to work with and unpredictable. Gene and Eddie hung out on the bus together on the way to the Mastbaum Theatre gig, by the time they pulled up at the venue, the pair were tight. As well as Gene, Eddie started appearing on bills with Chuck Berry, The Everly Brothers and Roy Orbison and getting more and more face time with the local radio DJs who were spinning his record. The radio guys were important to a rising star like Eddie. His job when he met the DJs was to be as nice as pie and try to convince them to spin him some more. Ever the courteous, well brought up young man, the DJs Eddie didn't get to meet in person he made sure he called on the telephone to introduce himself and charm his way to some airplay. It wasn't a hard sell, Eddie was personable, funny and polite, the records he was making were getting better and better and he was starting to tell whoever would listen that he was serious about this, and that he was after success.

Touring started to become what Eddie did. Nights at home with the family in Priory Street got fewer and further between

MOVIE ROLES ROCK EDDIE COCHRAN TO DISC STARDOM

BORN in Oklahoma City on October 3, 1938, Eddie Cochran began his career by singing and playing the guitar for local civic organisations and school dances. After moving to California in 1953, he soon built up a big local reputation.

Unlike many rock 'n' roll stars, he is an excellent guitarist and plays the instrument on all of his records. In California he became very popular among recording artists for his ability with the guitar and played the accompaniment for several big artists at their recording sessions.

It was in the studios that he met Jerry Capehart, who convinced him that he should try for a recording contract of his own. This was soon accomplished when Si Waronker and Jack Ames, of Liberty Records, heard Eddie sing and play.

His first disc for Liberty, "Sittin' In The Balcony," was acclaimed an overnight hit. He has since toured with all of the top shows in the States and worked such popular clubs as the Sands Hotel in Las Vegas.

He has also made many TV appearances on the major network shows in between his picture commitments in Hollywood.

AND HERE'S A SPECIAL MESSAGE FROM EDDIE

THANKS a million! That's the only thing I could think of to say when I heard that my "C'Mon Everybody" recording had been so successful in the British Isles.

I believe that some of you liked my earlier releases like "Sittin' In The Balcony" and "Twenty Flight Rock," and I was really thrilled when my "Summertime Blues" disc appeared in your charts a few months ago—especially as it was wintertime when it happened!

But as for having a song right up there in your Top Ten — gee, that's more than I ever dreamed could happen to me.

"Twenty Flight Rock" was the number I sang in Twentieth Century's "The Girl Can't Help It," which starred Jayne Mansfield, and I guess I owe a lot to that first appearance in movies.

Soon afterwards I was called on by Warner Brothers for a leading rôle in their picture, "Untamed Youth," alongside Mamie Van Doren. Boy, I sure get some cute leading ladies, don't I?

My latest movie — it's the biggest part I've had to date—is "Bop Girl," which was produced by Howard Koch of Bell-Air Productions. I hope you'll be seeing it on your side of the Atlantic real soon.

These days I'm devoting all my time to my career. I take my work in motion pictures very seriously. Acting is something that appeals to me in a big way and I hope the opportunity comes along to play some really good character rôles.

For this reason I'm looking forward to my next picture in which I play the part of a young teenager — a heavy dramatic rôle in which I don't do any singing at all.

I guess some of you would like to know a few details about my private life. Well, I'm the youngest of five children and the only member of the family who has chosen the entertainment field as a profession.

That makes me the baby of the family. It's something I just have to accept, although I'm not really the type of guy that likes to be babied.

I'm not married and don't have any special girl. I like to date several different girls.

My favourite hobbies are shooting and collecting guns. Unlike most youngsters of today, my favourite car isn't a sports model or a convertible, but a station wagon. No doubt that fits in with the rest of my character, for I like to dress very casually and I'm not too happy in big crowds.

I'd like to take this opportunity of thanking all the fans in Britain who've given me such wonderful support. I only hope that in the future, as my career grows, I'll be able to continue making the kind of records you like and the motion pictures you prefer.

Maybe it won't be too long before I can fix a trip to Britain and say "hello" to all of you in person.

June, 1959

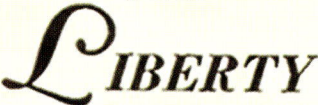

'Sittin' In The Balcony': Eddie's got a hit on his hands.

as he zigzagged from state to state and stage to stage. Despite all of the work he was doing and the acclaim he was beginning to receive, Eddie didn't yet have the bank balance to match. Brother Bob got into some financial trouble while Eddie was out on the road and it looked like his family might lose their house through not keeping up payments on it. All brother Bob needed was six hundred dollars to keep the wolves from the door but when he asked Eddie to lend him the money to get him out of trouble, Eddie didn't have it. When he did have some downtime, Eddie liked to listen to Amos 'n' Andy, a radio comedy set in first Chicago, then New York, which featured Eddie's favourite character, Kingfish. Eddie liked to laugh and Amos 'n' Andy made him howl. His affection for the Kingfish character was so deep that he'd throw in some of the character's phrasing while he was singing. Although not really a big TV guy, one show that Eddie would try to catch, as would pretty much everyone around him, was Dick Clark's *American Bandstand*. *Bandstand* was important, it was one of the first shows to embrace rock'n'roll and feature it on a regular basis and one of the only places you could see its stars in action and put faces to the voices on the radio. *Bandstand*'s line-up regularly included black and white musicians performing for non-segregated audiences. It presented rock'n'roll as inclusive, it reflected where the kids were at and it helped to show what a new America might look like. Show host Dick Clark got his big break on *Bandstand* when the previous host was fired for drunk driving. Dick was clean-cut and wholesome, a reassuring presence for mom and dad as he introduced their offspring to a wild new world every weekday between three and five in the afternoon, just as the kids were getting home from school. Clark studied business at college and bought the lessons he learnt there into the world of TV and would go on to become one of the richest people within the industry and in the process earn himself a place in the rock'n'roll Hall of Fame. A spot on *Bandstand* could send a rising star supernova by putting them in front of every teenager in the country.

'Sittin' In The Balcony' did good business and blew some wind into Eddie's sails. The song was pretty straightforward, what made it special was Eddie's vocal take, the reverb, the rockabilly inflections and the guitar break where the whole song is transformed. The 6120 strains against the confines of the tune then busts it wide open and stamps Eddie Cochran all over it. It would be a while before Eddie would admit that 'Sittin' In The Balcony' wasn't his favourite song and he was surprised at it being a hit and that hearing the playbacks when he first cut the song was a disappointment. But the fans loved it, and as Eddie sold more records and broke more hearts, fan mail started arriving. It came slowly at first, then in a wave so large it was going to need someone to manage it. Alice and sister Gloria took on the task of setting up and running The Eddie Cochran Fan Club and made sure that Eddie's wish that every fan who wrote to him should receive a reply was granted. Eddie played an active role in the fan club, he'd write back in person as often as he could and he started signing off his notes the same way, with 'Don't forget me. Eddie Cochran'. Despite having a top 20 single and all that came with it, Eddie still put the music first and when he wasn't on the road or recording himself, he could still be found working on sessions for other people.

Eddie took his fans, and his fan club, very seriously.

508 East 45 Street
Brooklyn 3, N. Y.
June 14, 1959

Hi Eddie,

Received your letter last week, but just haven't had the time to answer it. I'm so very sorry. Please forgive me?

We've gotten about 15 new members this past week. If memberships keep multiplying at this rate, we may ~~be~~ be able to have a buletin printed up by the end of the summer.

Eddie, I was thinking that it might be a good idea if you had one national fan club and have the other fan clubs as chapters. Then you could have one bulletin printed up with the news of each chapter printed in it. Of course this is entirely up to you, but if you give me the names and addresses of the other presidents I could write to them and get their opinion of it.

By the ~~w~~ way, what do you think of honorary members? That is asking famous people of the sports and entertainment worlds to join our club for you.

EDDIE COCHRAN FAN CLUB
Pres. Carol Bednar

List of Members:

1. Carol Bednar (Pres.) R.D. #1 Center Valley, Pa.
2. Carol Zerfass (V.P.) R.D. #1 Center Valley, Pa.
3. Virginia Woodring R.D. #1 Center Valley, Pa.
4. Pat Dekrane R.D. #1 Center Valley, Pa.
5. Sally Danenhower R.D. #1 Center Valley, Pa.
6. Sandy Bauer R.D. #1 Center Valley, Pa.
7. Mariann Kniess R.D. #1 Center Valley, Pa.
8. Dolores Sietenwalner R.D. #1 Center Valley, Pa.
9. David Bednar Jr. R.D. #1 Center Valley, Pa.
10. Cecilia Bednar R.D. #1 Center Valley, Pa.
11. Mary Ann Harmony R.D. #1 Center Valley, Pa.
12. Sandy Deutsch 836 W. Station Avenue, Coopersburg, Pa.
13. Karen Brobst Star Route, Coopersburg, Pa.
14. Ella Mae Ingram N. Main St. Coopersburg, Pa.
15. Carol Erdman State St. Coopersburg, Pa.
16. Cathy Hofstetter 336 Sandis St. Coopersburg, Pa.
17. Judy Frankenfield R.D. #4 Bethlehem, Pa.
18. Suzanne Spang R.D. #3 Bethlehem, Pa.
19. Joyce Werkheiser R.D. #1 Center Valley, Pa.
20. Kitty Lynette Herbster Star Route Limeport, Pa.

c/o Mr. John J. Havira DAC
U. S. Army Trans. Ip. T.O.D.
A.P.O. 331, c/o P.M., S.F., Calif.

Dear Eddie,
Hi! Gee! Thanks for the picture you sent me. It's real nice of you to send me that picture with your autograph. I was so overjoyed when I received it.

Please, Eddie! Tell me if you have any fan club. If you do, I would like to join. I haven't heard any of your records yet, but, I saw you in "The Girl Can't Help It." You were cute! And, if you have any list of your records, would you mind sending me a copy? I want to make sure I buy all your records. Please, Pretty Please, with lots of sugar on it, around it, above it and under it, Eddie! Gee, Thanks.

Well, so long for now! I just want to say Good Luck, Good Health, and God Bless you, Now and forever, Eddie.

Thanks again for that picture you sent me! Sweet Dreams!

Always sincere,
Josephine
(Havira)

Rock'n'roll is a business. Gloria and Shrimper are running the fan club, but Eddie's answering as many letters as he can and writing all the cheques.

(This page) The Third Annual Chicago Youth Rally on 28 April 1957, with Bernice (left) and Marilyn (right).

(Opposite) More from The Third Annual Chicago Youth Rally. Eddie seen meeting fan Chuck Baker in the top image.

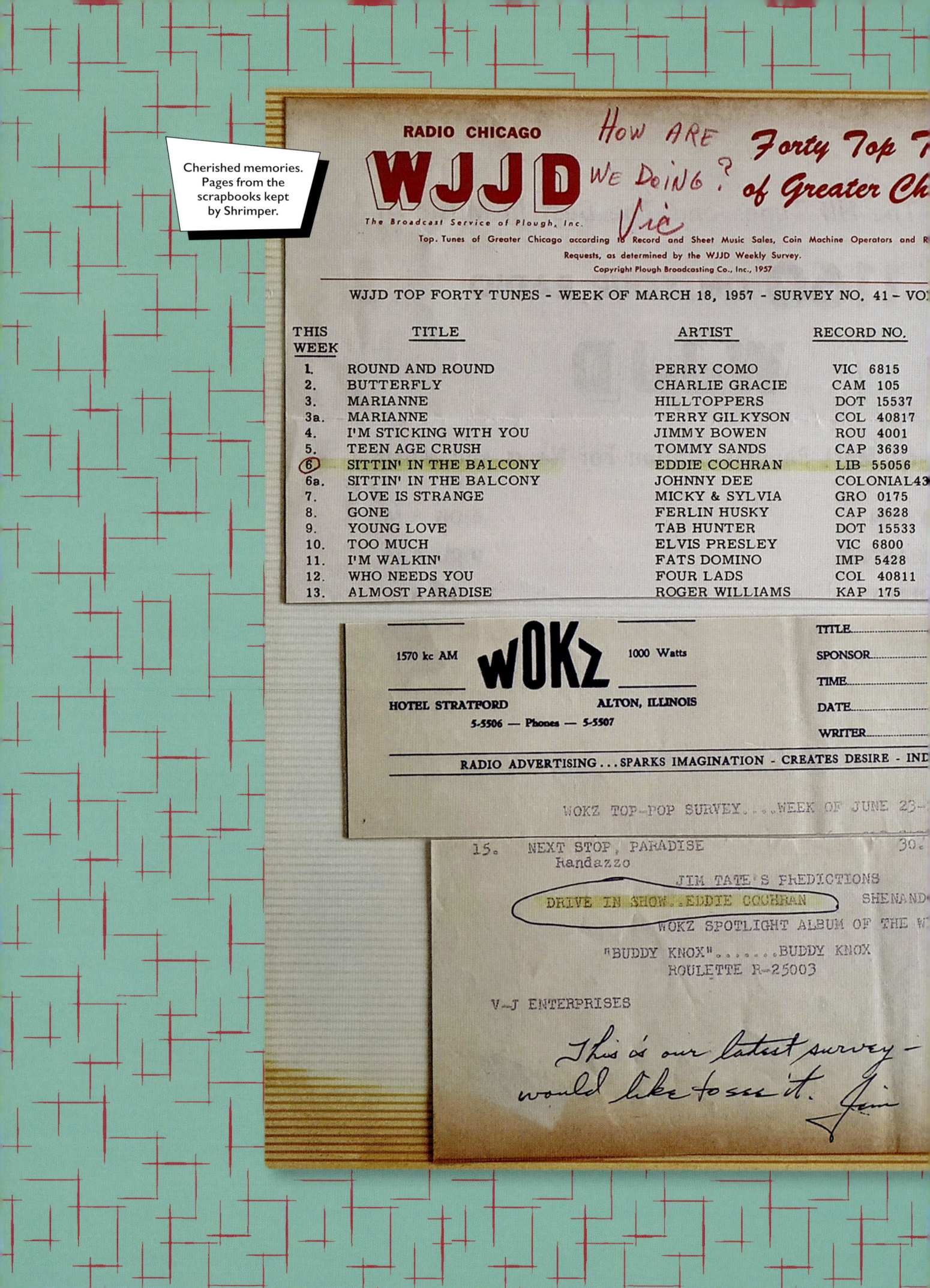

Cherished memories. Pages from the scrapbooks kept by Shrimper.

Eddie and Mamie find their rhythm on *Untamed Youth*.

Chapter Eleven

IN MAY OF 1957, the bad-girl movie *Untamed Youth* got its cinematic release. While the film may not have had the impact and slick production values of *The Girl Can't Help It*, it did work as another way of getting Eddie out there, of having him perform in drive-ins and theatres up and down the country and add to the growing perception that Eddie Cochran was a star on the rise. *Untamed Youth* starred another archetypal fifties bombshell starlet, Mamie Van Doren, in the lead role. Where *The Girl Can't Help It* plays in bright jewel colours, *Untamed Youth* is a far grittier black and white affair. Eddie plays Bong in the film, he gets to say a few lines and perform a number, 'Cotton Picker', in a field. The movie's star and poster girl, Mamie, had made her first movie back in 1951 and *Untamed Youth* was to be her thirteenth. Her resume included her appearance as the unforgettable Irma Bean in the 1955 B-movie classic, *Running Wild*, which had played as a double feature when it was sent out to theatres and drive-ins with another so-bad-it's-good movie, *Tarantula*.

Mamie and Eddie got on, they hit it off. They met before shooting started on the movie when they were introduced by the director Howard Koch and pretty soon Eddie started hanging out with Mamie and her husband, the band leader Ray Anthony. Ray was known to hate the new rock'n'roll, but whatever his feelings were about it, they didn't get in the way of his spending time with Eddie. Eddie and Mamie started working in the studio together, recording four numbers for the *Untamed Youth* soundtrack. They recorded 'Salamander', 'Go, Go, Calypso!', 'Rollin' Stone' and the stand out number, credited to four songwriters, including Cochran and Capehart, 'Oo Ba La Baby'. The songs were then released as an EP and distributed to radio stations to help push the movie. Hollywood being Hollywood, people soon began to speculate that the blond bombshell and the hot new rocker were making beautiful music together in more ways than one.

There was another persistent rumour on the set of *Untamed Youth*, this time that Eddie was getting close with an actress named Jeanne Carmen who was playing Lillibet in the film. Jeanne was vivacious and beautiful and came with a backstory that read like a movie script. At age 13, tired of picking cotton beneath the harsh southern sun, Jeanne had run away from home. She'd wound up in New York where she got work as a burlesque dancer in Bert Lahr's big show and posed as a pinup model for the popular girly magazines of the day. As well as the bump n' grind of burlesque and the stag shoots, Jeanne supplemented her income by working as a trick-shot golf hustler in Las Vegas. The worlds she moved in brought her into contact with connected guys, it was 'Handsome' Johnny Roselli, a mob guy with movie connections, who first introduced her to Frank Sinatra, and Frank who got her out to Hollywood. Once in Tinsel Town, Jeanne went on to appear in twenty movies. There weren't many women like Jeanne Carmen around in the mid-fifties. She was a strong, independent, smart and beautiful trailblazer. She smouldered on screen and took her acting seriously enough to study with Strasberg while she was in New York. That Eddie fell for Jeanne, while at the front of the stages he's playing on groups of pretty girls are starting to gather, tells us a lot about him, about how he was starting to become attracted to cool, powerful, accomplished women, the same women that other young men found intimidating and hard to approach. Eddie liked Jeanne for real, even though that meant keeping their relationship under wraps and off Mamie Van Doren's radar. One time while the pair were leaning against a car, necking on the studio lot, Mamie sashayed by and would have seen Eddie and Jeanne in love's young embrace had they not ducked down behind the car and waited for the bombshell starlet to pass. Eddie got romantic with Jeanne, he sent her bunches of red roses surrounding a single yellow flower at their centre. When the pair of them took part in a set-piece dance scene in the film featuring a whole bunch of cast members, they situated themselves at the back of the shot and got caught up in their own bump and grind routine, not caring whether or not they made the final cut.

Eddie was also romantically linked to another actress from *Untamed Youth*, Yvonne Lime, though this appears to be far more a love affair of convenience, confected in-house as a PR stunt and printed up in the teen mags in the hope that it would sell more cinema tickets and records. Yvonne had dated Elvis for a while and over an illustrious career lit up the screen in some of the most iconic b-movies of the time. You can see her in *Dragstrip Riot*, *High School Hellcats*, *Speed Crazy* and *Teenage Werewolf*. The teen magazine *Dig!* ran a story on the movie's release which romantically linked Eddie to Yvonne, illustrating the piece with pictures of Eddie and Yvonne cosily working together in the studio. Eddie and Yvonne did spend time making music together, this much we know for sure, and of their sessions a single song remains, 'Ting-A-Ling Telephone'. Eddie was learning the game and seeing that the constant rumours that were being whispered and printed about Eddie and the Hollywood movie girls he may or may not have been dating were doing no harm to his growing reputation and public profile.

Upon its release it soon became obvious that *Untamed Youth* wasn't the movie that *The Girl Can't Help It* was, Eddie had struck

(This page) Eddie with Yvonne Lime at Liberty Custom Recorders on 15 May 1957 during a publicity shoot.

(Opposite) Eddie hangs out with the *Untamed Youth* crowd. From left to right: Don Burnett and Lori Nelson, Yvonne Lime, Jeanne Carmen, Eddie, Valerie Reynolds, John Russell and Mamie Van Doren.

lucky with his first Hollywood outing but if he wanted to pursue his dream of chart success and Hollywood stardom, he was going to have to work for it. Initial reviews of the movie weren't great but they didn't stop it from reaching its intended audience, it became popular at drive-ins up and down the country and further propelled the name Eddie Cochran into the public consciousness. At Twentieth Century Fox, movie executives started to take an interest in Eddie, no doubt aware of the box-office power of Elvis Presley and wondering whether they might be able to snag a crowd-pleasing movie rocker of their own. After some acting classes from Ben Bart, Eddie attended what he thought would be a simple audition, keen to prove his potential and get some more time on the silver screen. Eddie spent half a day shooting with Sandra Dee on the Fox lot, then attended a screening of the footage with Jerry and a roomful of studio execs. The execs liked what they saw on the screen but weren't too enamoured of what they heard when Eddie declared to those present how 'motherfuckin' good' his audition looked on the big screen. Eddie's faux-pas notwithstanding, he landed a part in a Paul Newman and Joanne Woodward movie called *Rally Round the Flag, Boys*.

The part was small and Eddie had a few good lines but at a family conference at Priory Street the Cochrans weren't happy with Eddie taking the role. The feeling was that the role wasn't big enough for Eddie, that following his two recent screen outings it was a step back and that Jerry had let him down. Mistrust and resentment of Jerry Capehart had been growing in the Cochran household for a while, they wanted the best for Eddie, the best movie parts, the best record deals and the best gigs and felt that as a manager, Jerry was falling short, that he wasn't spending enough time getting Eddie where he should be and as a result, Eddie wasn't receiving the showbiz offers he deserved. Jerry tried to explain that although the part was small, the role was good and an appearance in a film like *Rally Round the Flag, Boys* would get Eddie noticed by a new section of the movie-going audience, that it would widen his appeal and lead somewhere. Jerry's protestations were for naught, Eddie bowed to the wishes of his family and called Fox to let them know he wouldn't be appearing in the movie. Always learning, Eddie had taken note of the make-up they used in auditions and movies and dug the way it looked, so he began to wear a little himself for photoshoots and gigs.

YOUTH TURNED 'ROCK-N-ROLL' WILD AND THE 'PUNISHMENT' FARM THAT MAKES THEM WILDER!
Kids gone wrong --and the 'Farm's' disgraceful penal abuse!
"UNTAMED YOUTH"
MAMIE VAN DOREN
LORI NELSON
JOHN RUSSELL · DON BURNETT

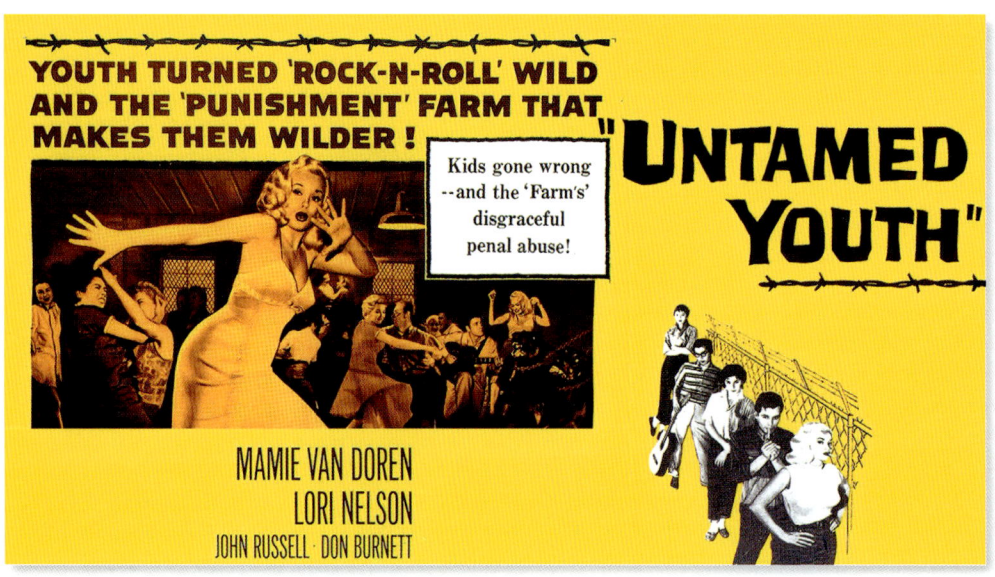

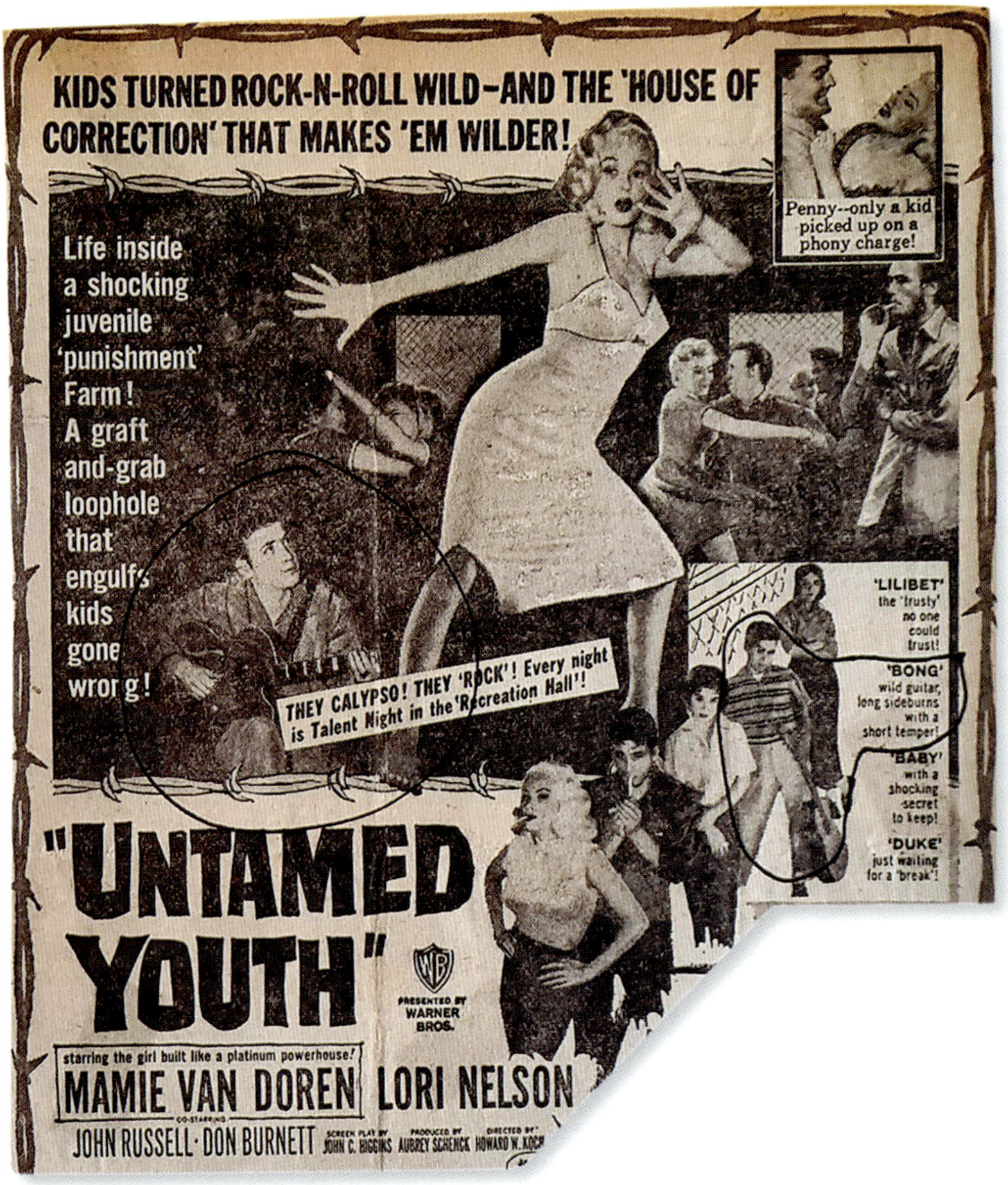
KIDS TURNED ROCK-N-ROLL WILD—AND THE 'HOUSE OF CORRECTION' THAT MAKES 'EM WILDER!
Penny--only a kid picked up on a phony charge!
Life inside a shocking juvenile 'punishment' Farm! A graft and-grab loophole that engulfs kids gone wrong!
THEY CALYPSO! THEY 'ROCK'! Every night is Talent Night in the 'Recreation Hall'!
'LILIBET' the 'trusty' no one could trust!
'BONG' wild guitar, long sideburns with a short temper!
'BABY' with a shocking secret to keep!
'DUKE' just waiting for a 'break'!
"UNTAMED YOUTH"
PRESENTED BY WARNER BROS.
starring the girl built like a platinum powerhouse!
MAMIE VAN DOREN
LORI NELSON
CO-STARRING
JOHN RUSSELL · DON BURNETT
SCREEN PLAY BY JOHN C. HIGGINS
PRODUCED BY AUBREY SCHENCK
DIRECTED BY HOWARD W. KOCH

Hand-written musical score for 'CottonPicker', the song Eddie performed in *Untamed Youth*.

68 Pennsylvania avenue
Jamestown, New York
May 6, 1957

Liberty Records
Hollywood, California

Gentlemen:

I would like to know if Eddie Cochran has recorded "Too Tired To Rock" which he sung in "The Girl Can't Help It". If he has I would like to know if it would be possible to order it from your company.

Regards,
Gary Delair
68 Pennsylvania ave.
Jamestown, New York

816 Phoenix St.
South Haven, Michigan.
March 7, 1957

Dear Eddie,
    I finally found out what your address is so I could write you a fanm letter. I have wanted to write to you for a picture of you ever sice I saw "The Girl Can't Help It".
    Would you please send me a real cool picture of you? I would be glad to pay for it if there is any cost.
    I think you are the mostest to say the leastest. I just love to hear you sing and I wished you would have a T.V. show of your own and would make some more movies.
    If you have time would you please write me a personal letter? If you do write to me please do it yourself and don't let a stodgy old (or young) secretary do it.
    Thank you very much.
    DIG YA LATER, ALLIGATOR!!!!!!!!

                              Love ya always,
                              Bobbi Higgs
                              Age: 15

P.S.
    B.B.H.C.Y.K.
       (Bye, Bye, Honey, Consider Yourself KISSED!!!!)
Extra P.S.
    How old are you and are you married?

TV RADIO MIRROR

RADIO MIRROR • AUG.

Eddie Cochran

NEW HOT SINGERS of 1957

WIN THIS ORIGINAL COVER PAINTING

ew Hot Singers of 1957

w Hot Singers of 1957

...hers irked Eddie Cochran—but
...n Hollywood he works hard with
...nger and songwriter Ray Stanley.

...uragements and approval help
...ger's style. Eddie Cochran,
...ma-born, Minnesota-reared
...who gave many teenagers
..."Sittin' in the Balcony," still
...at "that glee club deal." Says
...teacher didn't dig the music
...g. He gave me a bad time,
...nted me to sing all this long-
...was trying to teach me."
...dy knew how he wanted to
...brothers, sisters, dad and
...to hear me sing. We used to
...the house. Home singing is
...g."
...berant guitar player, he sat in
...dates of others. Song writer
...art, his personal manager,
...lo to Liberty Records with
...ght Rock"—"then they called
...d if I'd be kind enough to do
...movie 'The Girl Can't Help
...bout knocked me out. Every-
...real great to me." Acclaim
...ems: "You go all these places
...people are buttering you up
...screaming and all. It's not
...p your feet on the ground,
...he has worked for his suc-
...o thinks he's lucky. "I feel
...about some who have been
...than me, and trying hard,
...ake it." Eddie, young as he
...ke a long view. "We're just
...le, so when this deal came
...we just looked at it as some-

Eddie did "Twenty Flight Rock" for Liberty, was then paged for movie role.

Chapter Twelve

IN MAY OF '57, Liberty Records put out Eddie's second solo single. This time they chose 'One Kiss', with 'Mean When I'm Mad' on the flipside. Eddie, by now as comfortable in the studio as he was at home, got into character for 'Mean When I'm Mad', he threw some snarl and growl into his vocal performance and of the two songs it's the flipside that gets us most in touch with Eddie. At this point in his career, Eddie seemed to be recording some songs because other people thought that they positioned him where they thought he ought to be, and others because they far more accurately reflected where he was. Si Waronker liked some bang for his buck and was always in the market for relatively cheap but effective ways to get noticed in a market which was getting more and more crowded by the day. For 'One Kiss' he sent out a postcard to Eddie's fans letting them know of the single's imminent release and splashed out on a full colour picture sleeve, confident that the song was bound to do well given the success of 'Sittin' In The Balcony'. It didn't. 'One Kiss' didn't even chart. It was a shame. Had more people bought the record then more people would have heard 'Mean When I'm Mad' on the B-side. Things had been going so right, the movie deals and the chart success, so the disappointing performance of 'One Kiss' hit hard, it stalled momentum and forced all concerned to stop for a beat and reconsider. Nonetheless, the show had to go on and by the end of May, Eddie was hard at work on his first album, *Singin' To My Baby*.

The songs chosen for *Singin' To My Baby* reflected perfectly the slightly muddled approach to how those around him wanted to present Eddie Cochran. They wanted to distance themselves from comparisons with Elvis while at the same time capitalise on Elvis's success, they wanted to distance Eddie from the rock'n'roll that made him a star in the first place yet keep hold of Eddie's growing rock'n'roll fanbase. They were still hedging their bets and building in some insurance that if this rock'n'roll thing didn't last then Eddie wouldn't be tied to closely to it. But by then it was too late, rock'n'roll and Eddie Cochran were one and the same, it was just that some of the people around him hadn't realised it yet.

Eddie returned to Gold Star Studio B to record the album. By now he was familiar with the studio, he knew what it was capable and how to make it work for him.

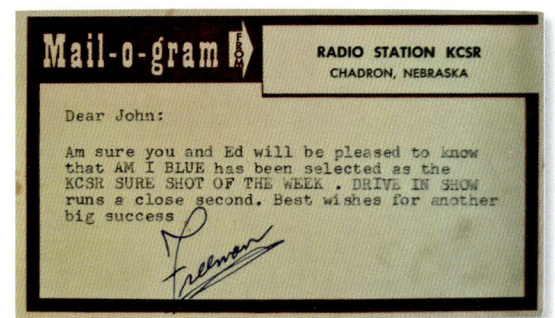

Guybo came along to play bass and the Johnny Mann Chorus came along to provide backing vocals. Eddie's erstwhile mentor, musical partner and manager, Jerry Capehart, was credited with co-writing a quarter of the album and Si Waronker essentially produced the record, as he did all of the early Liberty albums, getting a say in everything from its instrumentation to its track listing. *Singin' To My Baby* opens with Eddie's hit, 'Sittin' In The Balcony', as track one side one. Next comes a re-recorded version of 'Completely Sweet' where Eddie and Guybo can be heard having some fun as they make their magic. 'Completely Sweet' is followed by a trio of slower numbers, 'Undying Love', 'I'm Alone Because I Love You' and 'Lovin' Time', where Eddie gets to put the 6120 down and break out his ukulele. Side one finishes with 'Proud Of You', a song obviously chosen to highlight Eddie's ability to create good quality, unthreatening pop. Side two of *Singin' To My Baby* opens with 'Mean When I'm Mad' followed by 'Stockings and Shoes'. A couple of down tempo numbers in the shape of 'Have I Told You Lately That I Love You' and 'Tell Me Why' take up tracks 3 and 4 before the album ends on Cradle Baby and 'One Kiss'. As well as the songs intended to wind up on the album, Eddie also used the Studio B album sessions to record 'Drive-In Show' and Shrimper's favourite, 'Am I Blue', where Eddie again got to break out his ukulele, which were slated as his next Liberty single release.

Eddie was 18 years old and already a seasoned professional with a hit behind him and his first album in the can. Turning 18 had meant that he could finally get hold of his driving licence, albeit two years later than everyone else. Eddie had ensured that there might be a problem being issued a licence when he'd been pulled over for driving underage prior to his 16th birthday and it was decreed that as punishment, he'd have to wait two years longer to get his licence. Whatever the opinion of the material chosen to make up *Singin' To My Baby*, what is undeniable is that Eddie sounded comfortable and assured throughout and on one level the record did exactly what it was supposed to do, it showed Eddie's range and ability and proved that he could turn his hand to more than rock'n'roll. But trying to make Eddie all things to all people was a strategy that was, in truth, starting to fail. The poor sales of 'Drive-In Show' upon its release compounded the disappointment of 'One Kiss''s failure to chart.

Little Richard

Although it did better than its predecessor and made it to number eighty-two on the *Billboard 100*, Eddie's second flop in a row was a tough blow to take for Eddie and his team. They needed to reconsider, they needed to look at who Eddie was rather than who they wanted him to be, and they needed to let Eddie be Eddie.

By the end of summer 1957, rock'n'roll was a worldwide phenomenon. The word had spread and demand had grown and in order to fill it over in Australia, an established promoter with a solid history of bringing American acts to Australia by the name of Lee Gordon had put together what he called *The Big Show*, and booked Eddie to play it. There was trepidation about the tour in the Cochran household. When Johnny Rook went to Priory Street for a farewell dinner before Eddie left it became obvious that Eddie wasn't happy at all about the amount of time the flight took and that Alice didn't like the idea of her boy working halfway around the world. Eddie would be on the road with Alis Lesley, Johnny O'Keefe, Little Richard and Gene Vincent. The tour was pretty wild from the first date it played and Eddie threw himself into the backstage and onstage shenanigans and had all the fun he could. Onstage, he and Gene were competing to see who could do the longest set and put on the craziest show while they were up there and Little Richard was being torn to shreds by adoring fans every night. Backstage, the musicians, Eddie included, were taking full advantage of the hospitality offered by the local fans from whichever town they were playing and raising hell every chance they got. The musicians hit a lingerie store and bought a bunch of panties, each emblazoned with a different day of the week and began throwing them out into the crowds of screaming girls during the encore. The tour got wilder as it hit Brisbane, Melbourne and Wollongong and Sydney where the whole thing suddenly came to a grinding, crashing halt when Little Richard saw a sign and renounced rock'n'roll and declared that from that point on he would devote his life to the Lord. Richard's route to rock'n'roll had the church tradition in it, the gospel songs and the danger of sin and, just like Jerry Lee Lewis, Richard struggled with his relationship with God as he made his living playing the Devil's music. Little Richard was implacable, he'd seen a fireball lighting up the sky, his mind was made up and the die was cast, the world was ending and he needed baptism back in his homeland before it did. No amount of telling Richard that maybe what he saw was the Sputnik that Russia had just launched into space would change his mind. He pulled the four diamond rings that rock'n'roll had bought him from his fingers and tossed them into the Hunter River in the hope that God was watching and his sacrifice would be duly noted up in heaven. Then he flew home two weeks early and started the process that would see him ordained as The Reverend Richard Penniman.

The hole that opened up in Eddie's schedule thanks to Little Richard's religious awakening didn't stay open for long. No sooner had he touched down back in the US in October 1957 than he was booked to appear on *The Biggest Show Of Stars For '57*, a tour that included Chuck Berry, The Everly Brothers, Fats Domino, Paul Anka and Buddy Holly. The tour was a grind, each act spending their forty plus days on the road waiting to get on stage, but once up there only being allotted enough time to get through three numbers at most. Eddie got close with Don and

Alis Lesley

Phil Everly on the tour, he struck up a friendship with Buddy Holly and discovered a mutual love of practical jokes with singer LaVern Baker. Phil Everly would later recall that Chuck Berry always liked to open the show so he could spend the rest of the evening hanging out at the soda machine, charming the local girls. To keep themselves amused the musicians on the tour starting gambling on dice games backstage. Money also started changing hands when bets were placed on how close Eddie would leave it to showtime bust through the door with Guybo and make his way to the stage. Eddie made the most of his late entrances, making a show of shrugging his overcoat from his shoulders as he made his way through the musicians and crew assembled backstage before greeting the audience and plugging in his 6120. Eddie was hitting the stage in his tweed jacket, necktie and slip-ons, eschewing showbiz flash and focussing on musical substance with his front curl falling as he rocked and him slicking it back between songs. He was picking up more media experience on the tour too, and his 2 November KCSR *Bandstand* interview with Freeman Hover, conducted while the tour was passing through Denver, has survived. Eddie spoke to Freeman from his hotel room, fresh from performing at the Denver Auditorium with Fats Domino, Clyde McPhatter, Lavern Baker, Frankie Lymon, Chuck Berry, Buddy Holly and The Crickets and Paul Anka. The next stop on the road was Wichita.

FH *Here's the boy that you've been hearing about, that they've been talking about, the lad that has the number eight tune on the KCSR top 10 this week… Eddie Cochran.*

After introducing Eddie, Freman wants to know about life on the road, about the travelling.

EC *On the shorter hops we have chartered buses and then for the longer hops, anything from two to five hundred miles, then we fly…*

FH *I bet it takes a lot out of you doesn't it?*

EC *Yes Sir it really does, you get pretty tired…*

FH *How long have you been in the business?*

EC *I've been in the business just about five years.*

FH *How'd ya start out? Can you give us a little bit of a rundown?*

EC *I was a guitar player and I was playing y'know record dates, out in Hollywood, I'd moved out there from Oklahoma City. I was doing one of these record dates one day and a fella walked in there and it was just in between takes so I was just sitting there just picking on my guitar y'know for my own amazement. He walked in and he wanted to know if I wanted to make a movie as a singer and I told him 'yeah, I'll do it'.*

I hadn't done too much singing really you know, I went out and I cut a dub of a song called 'Twenty Flight Rock' and I took it over out to Twentieth Century Fox and they put me in The Girl Can't Help It.

73

Gene Vincent

Eddie seemed happy, comfortable and relaxed in the interview and used it to further build the myth that he was an Okie rather than a Minnesota boy. He's just played a show to twelve thousand people and in the next room are Buddy Holly and Jimmy Bowen. They've stolen Eddie's baritone ukulele and Eddie wants it back.

Over at Liberty Records, Si Waronker needed a new Eddie Cochran single. The label needed hits, there was way too much money going out and not nearly enough coming in. The financial vultures had started swirling in the skies above Liberty Records and they were getting ready to swoop. Waronker and Liberty decided that finally, the song that had got Eddie noticed in the first place should be his next release. The version of 'Twenty Flight Rock' which Liberty put out had been re-recorded at a Gold Star session earlier in the year when it was decided that a less gritty version of the song would be more palatable and appeal to a wider audience. It wasn't and it didn't. By the time 'Twenty Flight Rock' was released the song was, in the fast moving world of early rock'n'roll, old news, *The Girl Can't Help It* had been and gone from cinemas and the song's moment had passed.

All in all, Waronker and Liberty Records were on the hook for almost a million dollars in debts and unpaid taxes as 1957 started drawing to a close. When the dire state of the company finances were revealed, Waronker was as shocked as anyone and left wishing he'd been way more selective when employing sales managers and choosing business partners. Sales figures had been altered, books had been cooked and when the full extent of Liberty's financial woes came to light, Waronker faced the choice of whether to fold it up and walk away or stay and fight for his company. He stayed and fought and assured Eddie that as long as he had a record label, Eddie Cochran's music would have a home. Waronker needed money fast to plug the hole left by corruption and incompetence, pressing plants were threatening that until they settled what they already owed, Liberty wouldn't be able to press up new records, so Si hit the phone and started doing the deals that would save his company. Within three days he raised $80,000, bought out his partner's 20 per cent share, fired the in-house number cruncher and made an arrangement to pay off the pressing plants over the coming eighteen months. As well as firing, Waronker did some hiring too, and took on business whizz Al Bennett who was looking for a new gig having recently left Dot Records.

Eddie Cochran

March 12, 1957
P.O. Box 95
Wahoo, Nebr.

Dear Eddie ~

I got your letter and picture today. I'm going to Omaha tomorrow so I will try to get your new record.

I know several Disc Jockey's in Tampa and St. Petersburg, Florida, to see how you are doing down South. Thats where I'm orginally from.

I'm looking forward to seeing your latest picture.

KEEp working but not too hard.

I think your great.
Sincerely
Martha
A.
Cream

Judy Clark
8338 Torresdale Ave,
Phila., Pa.

Dear Eddie,

Naturally you don't remember me. But I was one of the many girls who got your autograph at bandstand, Feb. 19. In fact I got two of them. At that time you gave me this address to obtain a picture. So — could you please send me one. My address is above. Also, can you give me this information?

Chapter Thirteen

FOR THOSE AROUND Eddie, 1958 started with a big sigh of relief when Waronker's faith and determination to save Liberty paid off. The label released David Seville's obstinately weird novelty tune 'Witch Doctor', it went on to be a number one smash and thanks to Si Waronker and Al Bennett, Liberty was saved.

On 12 January 1958, Eddie hit the studio with Guybo and a drummer named Earl Palmer and laid down 'Jeannie, Jeannie, Jeannie'. Earl had worked with Fats Domino and Little Richard and had the sound and the feel Eddie was looking for. By this time, Eddie was three flops away from his last big hit so the pressure was on to find a song that would re-establish him as a serious contender. The song he chose, 'Jeannie, Jeannie, Jeannie', had started life as 'Johnny, Johnny, Johnny', and was written by married songwriting partners George Motola and Rickie Page. Eddie, Guybo and Earl took the song, hung it upside down until the change fell out of its pockets and made it 100 per cent Eddie Cochran. It wasn't an easy session. Guybo's girl, Marilyn, finally tired of the endless takes in search of perfection and went and sat out in the parking lot. However difficult the session though, the results were worth it. 'Jeannie, Jeannie, Jeannie' barrels in like a wild train and doesn't let up until the final note. After all those slow songs and pop numbers Eddie can be heard relishing the freedom the song grants him and gives a vocal performance that is pure rock'n'roll gold; the Little Richard shows he'd caught in Australia had obviously had a big influence on Eddie and he sounds all the better for it. Liberty Records had learned their lesson the hard way where Eddie was concerned and, given the fact that the material they'd been choosing for him had been bombing, gave he and Jerry far freer rein when choosing what they would record. They put out 'Jeannie, Jeannie, Jeannie' and the schlockier B-side, 'Pocketful Of Hearts', in January but despite the positive feedback the song received upon release, it failed to translate to sales and the record stalled at number ninety-four. By the time February rolled around and Eddie was back on the road with The Coasters and Frankie Lymon and telling an interviewer that rock'n'roll was changing, but that the heavy beat will always be there, his latest single had all but disappeared. The Frankie Lymon gigs took Eddie and Jerry down to Hawaii where Eddie announced that if he weren't so into California, he'd make it his home. Eddie and Frankie started hanging out, one night they got drunk enough to think that pitching champagne glasses from the balcony of Eddie's room into the swimming pool below was a good idea. Glass after glass was hurled into the pool as their broken remains shimmered like diamonds in the water, then Frankie left and Eddie crashed out and got some sleep. The world Eddie woke up in was very different from that he had left the night before. There was a kid's swimming class due to take place in the pool and the hotel management weren't happy. There were also cops on their way, so Eddie and Jerry got on the first plane they could and didn't stick around to read the outraged editorials and sensationalised stories that described the debauched parties being held by the visiting rockers which began to appear the next day.

Undeterred by the sales of 'Jeannie, Jeannie, Jeannie' and buoyed by the reception he was still receiving on the road, Eddie headed back into the studio, this time Liberty Custom Recorders on La Brea, on 3 March, where he recorded the louche 'Teresa', possibly at the urging of those around him who were still more inclined to position him as an all-rounder than a flat-out rock'n'roller.

Eddie hadn't seen his buddy Gene since Australia, so when he got the call to come and help out on the sessions for 'A Gene Vincent Record Date', he headed straight over to the Capitol Records Studios in Hollywood. Eddie was good for Gene, he saw past the pain and the wildness and the unpredictability and the more time they spent together, the more the bond between them grew. Eddie knew the Blue Caps too so there was no resentment at his arrival and the bassy, R'n'B inspired backing vocals and the production ideas he provided helped to make Gene's next album what it was. Eddie got real friendly with all of The Blue Caps over the four days he spent recording with them (he took a day out to go record his own 'Summertime Blues') and hung out with them outside the studio too. He was a big admirer of Gene's drummer, Juvey Gomez's style. They shared a love of shoes and went shopping for crazy moccasins together. The Gene Vincent Capitol sessions produced the legendary 'Git It', a masterclass in rock'n'roll harmonising and the beauty of simplicity. The song was loose and precise at the same time, it was Eddie and his buddy Gene bringing the best out of each other and elsewhere in California a young Brian Wilson was listening intently. Gene's next gig once the record was finished was shooting for the movie *Hot Rod Gang*, a film that Jerry Capehart was working on as associate musical supervisor. Gene was staying in Hollywood with the Blue Caps over at the Knickerbocker Hotel. The hotel they'd been staying in prior to the Knickerbocker hadn't been able to keep up with the trashed rooms, the unholy noise and the endless parade of girls looking for a party, so they'd asked Gene and his motley crew to leave. Changing the venue didn't end the party though, it just moved it. Eddie was at the parties of course, as were Johnny Cash, Ricky Nelson and Lefty Frizzell.

Eddie in the Show Of Stars at the Civic Auditorium in Honolulu. Frankie Lymon topped the bill, with Eddie and The Coasters as the other two acts.

KASL

1240 KC

Mutual and Western Regional Networks

"THE VOICE OF NORTHEASTERN WYOMING"

NEWCASTLE, WYOMING

July 3, 1958

There once was a guy whose name was Ed,
He puts out records that knocks um' dead.
TERESA8s number two on KASL's chart,
SUMMERTIME BLUES is ready to start.

THE PICK OF THE WEEK it will make,
With KASL's help it's bound to take.
Good luck to you, and gee whiz dad,
I'm proud to say, YOUR A MIGHTY FINE LAD.

A SMASH IN K A S L KOUNTRY
America's New Teenage Idol
EDDIE COCHRAN
Singing
TERESA
Liberty records No. 55138
Give it a spin,
you'll like it . . .
Johnnie Rowe
K A S L Radio
Newcastle Wyoming

Getting the word out: Radio played a vital role in helping Eddie reach his audience.

"Teller Of Tales"
Robert Louis Stevenson Intermediate School — Feb. 28, 1958

Gladiola Hatchie and Cheryol Cromwell are all smiles, and why shouldn't they be, with Eddie Cochran's and Frankie Lymon's arms around them? Gladiola was MC and Cheryol was entertainment chairman for last Friday's freshmen canteen.

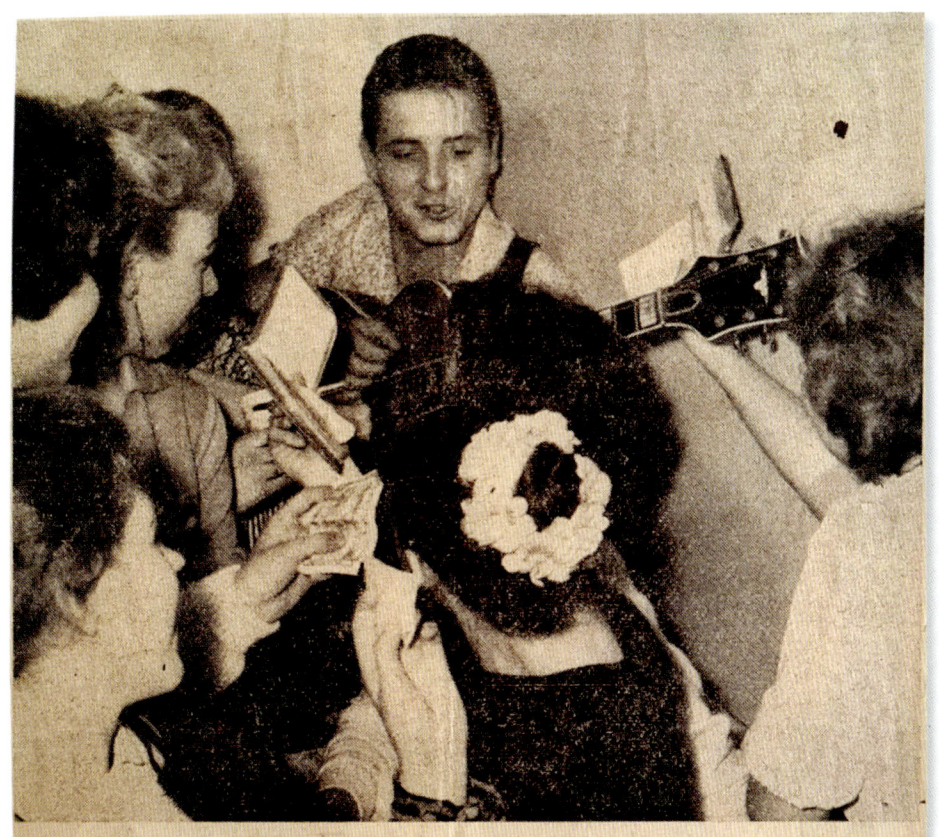

EAGER FANS BESIEGE ROCK 'N ROLL IDOL

Eddie Cochran got backed into a corner by eager fans during his debut here last night at Memorial Arena. The rock 'n roll idol from Oklahoma City, left Hollywood recently on a tour of B.C. Proceeds from the dance—attended by some 350 people—will go toward the Kelowna baseball team for improving Elks Stadium.
(Courier staff photo)— prints available

Rosemarie Mannino
4 LeBeau Place
Plainview, New York

3/10/58

Dear Eddie,
 How are you feeling? I'm fine and so is everyone here. Thank-you very much for answering again.
 I hope you enjoyed your tour. I'm sorry to say, but I didn't see you Jan. 29th on American Bandstand. That was a long time ago anyway.
 I heard your record — Eddie Jeanie Jeanie Jeanie and love it. I went to the store and looked for it but I couldn't find it so I didn't buy it.
 Thank-you kindly
 Love and kisses
 From one of your
 fans
 Rosemarie
 Mannino

MISSES;

Florence Arlene White
Helen Elva White
Adelaide Louise White

Phillips Road; Castleton; New York
R.F.D. #1; % Wm. White
April 8; 1958

Hello <u>Don't Forget Me</u> Eddie;;

    I know you said you were leaving for a tour of Hawaii, but I am sincerely hoping you are back now. I hope you had a wonderful time and I sure am sorry I couldn't get to see you when you played up in this kneck of the woods.

    In your last letter you asked me how I liked your version of the song " Jeannie; Jeannie; Jeannie," well; I personally think it was just great. I really liked it very much. I didn't hear the other song you mentioned as yet but I think it might be on the back side of the song Jeannie Jeannie Jeannie, is it?? If so, that is the reason I didn't hear the flip side. The radio dis-jockies only get stuck on one side and that is the only side of the record you hear for days. In this case it was the side you mentioned last Jeannie Jeannie Jeannie.

    I am sorry you had to cancel the picture but I hope you will be making one real soon. Which do you enjoy the most any how? The singing tours or making a motion picture? I'll bet you one thing, you make more money on your tours than you do from a picture, don't you????

    I sure hope you won't mind my writing now and than but you said to write when I have the spare time and that is what I am doing right now. Their isn't much to write about but I sure do hope you had a nice and long engagement in Hawaii and I'll be sending down a few lines from here now and than. Keep up your nice records and I'll be looking forward to seeing your next movie which I hope is real soon.

                                          Don't Forget Us;
                                Your old Fans;
                                The White Sister's from Castleton

Good Luck on your singing and hope you make a nice picture real soon.

Eddie and Sharon at Gold Star Studios.

Chapter Fourteen

IN 1958, THE business of rock'n'roll was still an almost exclusively male pursuit. The girls may have been buying the records but not many of them were yet writing or recording them, which made the maverick, mould-breaking Sharon Sheeley all the more impressive. Sharon was tall and cool, and by the time Eddie met her, her musical credentials were bona-fide. Following a brief stint as a teenage model she followed her musical dream all the way to California. 'Poor Little Fool', the song Sharon wrote as part of a school assignment when she was just 18, got to number one when Ricky Nelson, at the time a huge star, recorded it in 1958. Sharon was determined, talented and when she needed to be, she was crafty as hell. According to one version of the story, when Sharon first gave Ricky the song she told him her godfather had written it for Elvis, Ricky bought the line, recorded the song and didn't find out the truth of its origins, that it had been written by this girl, this kid, until it was way too late. Another version tells of Sharon staging a vehicle breakdown right in front of Ricky's house, and giving him the song while she waited for the tow-truck to arrive. Interviewed by Jim Pewter later in her life, Sharon revisited how she got Ricky to record her 'Poor Little Fool'. Pewter himself relayed the story Sharon had told him.

"She says I'm gonna have Ricky Nelson record this. So she drives over to where the Nelsons lived in Hollywood, drives up on their driveway, stops, and Ozzie comes out of the house and says what's the matter is something wrong? And she says Gee, I drove into this driveway by mistake. So Ricky comes out, Rick was rehearsing at the time in the house with James and everybody and she says I got a song here that I think you might be interested in. I wrote it for Elvis but instead of having Elvis do it I'd rather have Rick listen to it and see if he likes it… Ricky says well we'll listen to it, Sharon says well here's my phone number, just let me know. They work it out and it kinda fits into their rehearsal and when Ricky is about to record another album, they decide to put it on the album. …That song gets picked up by the DJs, they release it as a single and within a month or so it was number one on Billboard.*"*

Like Eddie, Sharon recognised the power of the media to help propel her to where she wanted to be and took full advantage of the attention she was suddenly garnering from the teen magazines as her song sat on top of the charts. It wouldn't be long before Sharon Sheeley was not only regularly appearing in the teen mags but writing her own column for one of them. Sharon knew her way around the scene and, at a Gene Vincent show she was attending with her sister, met a guy who took them backstage to meet the headliner. Sharon wasn't impressed, Gene was mean that night, like he was most nights. He was drunk and scathing and the Sheeley sisters had cut out early. Months later, Sharon and her sister were walking through Hollywood when they spotted the guy who'd introduced them to mean Gene. He spotted them too and called them in to come sit with him and hang out. When Sharon told him that she'd written Ricky's hit 'Poor Little Fool' and that she currently didn't have a manager, his ears pricked up and he got excited. He should manage her he said, he was in the business already. His name was Jerry he said, Jerry Capehart, and he managed a singer Sharon would have heard of, by the name of Eddie Cochran. Of course Sharon knew Eddie she told him, she'd met him before at an Everly Brothers show, but it had been a quick hi amongst a thousand others backstage and she would later find out that Eddie didn't even remember it happening. Sharon didn't mention to Jerry how she and her sister Mary Jo had stood outside of their local cinema when *The Girl Can't Help It* was playing and stared adoringly at Eddie. She also didn't mention that she'd told her sister that the beautiful guy in the poster was the one she was going to marry. When Jerry asked her if she had any songs that might suit Eddie she told that she had a ton that would be perfect for him, and then she ran home and started to write them.

Sharon's success with her songwriting debut had not gone unnoticed. Soon she was hanging out with a group of fellow hip young musicians and songwriters that included Rockabilly legend Johnny Burnette, The Everly Brothers, Phil Spector and Ricky Nelson and soon, Eddie Cochran. There are a few stories out there describing how Eddie met Sharon. In the first telling, the pair are introduced to one another backstage at the New York Paramount by Phil Everly, who may or may not have been Sharon's boyfriend at the time, which jives with Sharon's version. The second story was told in 1988 in a Levi's commercial called 'Eddie Cochran by Sharon Sheeley'. The action takes place on New Year's Eve, 1958. Eddie is going to the same party as Sharon, but which item from her knock-em-dead wardrobe should she pick to wear to maybe hang out with the one and only Eddie Cochran? She tries on dress after dress until alighting on her faithful blue jeans. She pairs the Levis with a sweatshirt, heads down to the party, makes her way through the small knot of girls done up to the nines and steals Eddie's heart with her unpretentious approach and her individuality. The Levi's commercial is a rock'n'roll fairy tale soundtracked by 'C'Mon Everybody'; in reality, when the pair first met, Sharon

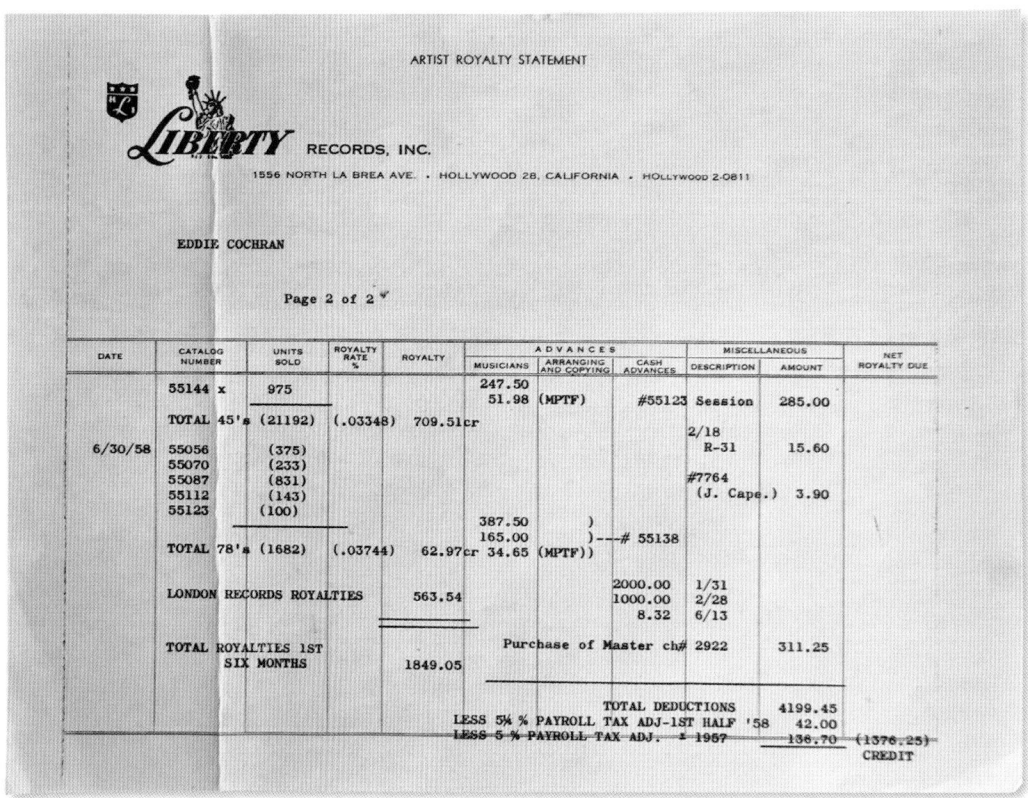

The bottom line: Liberty Records royalty statement.

was every bit as successful as Eddie, if not more so, and didn't need to pull on a pair of blue jeans to stand out in a crowd.

Eddie and Sharon's second meeting took place at Jerry's apartment. Sharon headed over expecting Jerry to be there but it was Eddie who answered the door and Jerry Capehart was nowhere to be seen. Eddie wanted to hear the song she'd written for him he said, and he handed her his 6120 and asked her to play it. Sharon's nerves kicked in. She wasn't a guitarist or a singer, she wrote songs, and here she was singing one, 'Love Again', for this famous stranger. Sharon's voice faltered and her notes slipped, she was out of tune and her tempo was drifting, she felt nervous and vulnerable singing like that so when Eddie did what he did with people all the time, when he teased her a little, she burst into tears and ran away. Eddie followed her and apologised. Two weeks later he was recording her song.

Liberty Records' faith in Eddie was strong, but the lack of success of his previous singles needed addressing. Si Waronker knew that Eddie was special, he knew that he had what it took and that his investment of time and money would eventually pay off, but they needed it to happen sooner rather than later. Sharon's 'Love Again' looked set to be Eddie's next single until Al Bennett took another listen to the song slated to go on the flipside. Bennett liked what he heard and decided that the B-side, a Jerry Capehart / Eddie Cochran composition called 'Summertime Blues', should be Eddie's next release. Years later, Jerry Capehart recounted how the song came into being.

'Eddie came by my apartment and we were having a rehearsal. The evening before, recording was scheduled the next day, so I said, "Well why don't we write something? Summer's coming, OK, there's never been a blues song written about summer so let's write a song", I told him, "call it 'Summertime Blues'." So Eddie says "Hey, you know, I've got this really great riff on the guitar…"

'Everything Eddie Cochran ever did in his life had to have humour in it or he wouldn't do it. For example, his favourite performer at that time was the Kingfish from the Amos 'n' Andy days and the little voice you can hear on Eddie's version of 'Summertime Blues' was really his salute to the Kingfish. I think 'Summertime Blues' was really indicative of Eddie's image with his fans. I think that song gave him his individuality.'

And just like that, one of the most important and well-loved pieces of music of the 20th century came into being. It was the right song at the right time, it was what Eddie wanted to say, how he wanted to say it and what the audience wanted to hear and it sounds as fresh today as it did the day it was recorded. 'Summertime Blues' was apparently written in a half hour over at Jerry's place the day before it was recorded in trusty Studio B over at Gold Star, it was the crack that broke the dam, the first in a brace of singles that would create and define the Eddie Cochran legend. 'Summertime Blues' was a stone cold killer. The public eventually agreed. When the song was released on 11 June it sold slowly and steadily at first, then began to fly off the shelves until it hit number eight on the chart by the end of September. The song should have proved to anyone at Liberty who still wasn't convinced that Eddie Cochran knew what he was doing and the less they tried to influence his image and his output, the more records he sold.

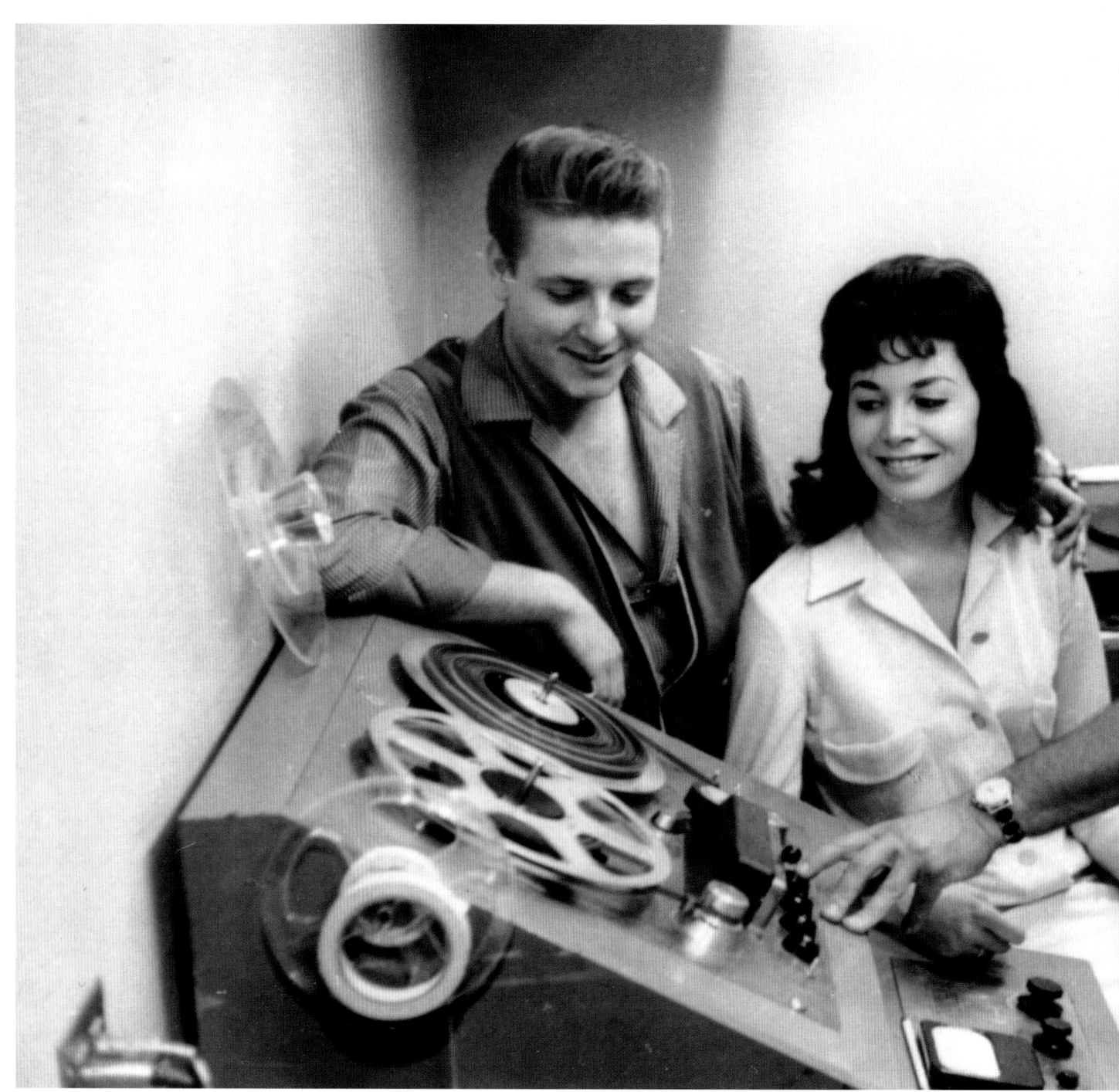

(Above) Eddie, Sharon and Stan Ross in the control booth at Studio B, Gold Star Studios.

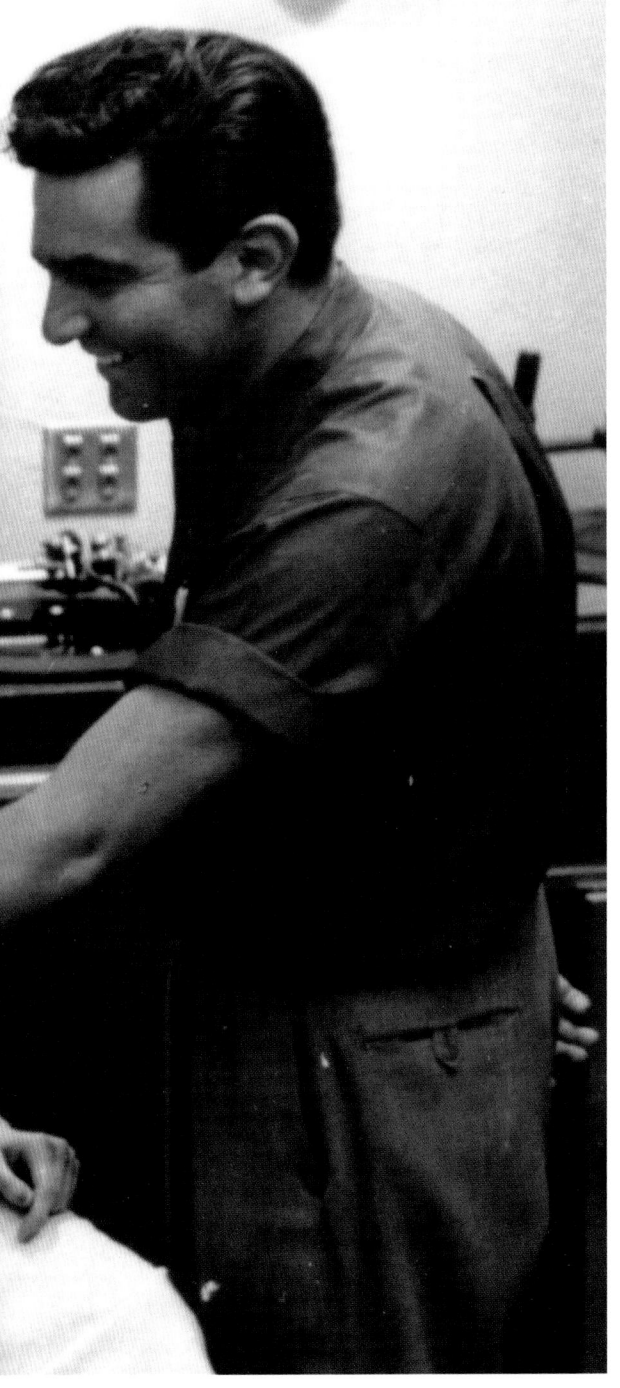

(Left) Jerry Capehart, Sharon, Eddie and Larry Levine.

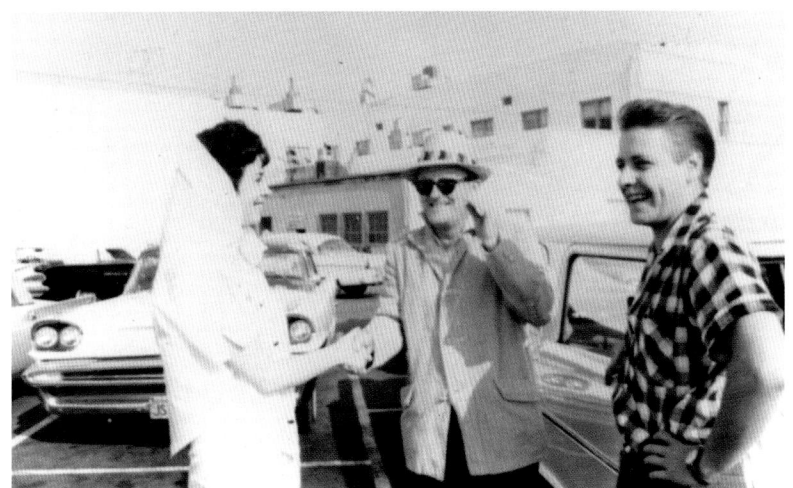

(Above) Eddie, Sharon and Billy Vaughn in the parking lot of Wallichs Music at Sunset and Vine, Los Angeles. Vaughn, as well as being a highly successful musician, was also an A&R man for Dot Records.

Chapter Fifteen

AFTER MONTHS OF disappointing sales, cancelled tours and money worries, Eddie and Liberty could breathe a sigh of relief. Suddenly Eddie was everywhere. The teen magazines were calling, they wanted heart-throb pics and the low-down on who Eddie was dating, the movie magazines and the music papers were calling too and suddenly all that practice that Eddie had garnered in front of TV cameras and journalists' notebooks was paying off. Anyone else might have bought into the hype and let their ego run away with them but Eddie was still Eddie, a teenage kid with a wicked sense of humour, a music student with a lot to learn. When he wasn't playing in front of theatres full of hollering fans, was back at home on Priory Street, getting spoiled by Shrimper, watching TV and sleeping in his own bed. Eddie also used what little downtime he had between touring and recording commitments to keep his hand in at the pursuits he'd loved since he was a kid back in Albert Lea. Eddie would go out into the desert, sometimes with his brothers or Johnny Rook or Bob Denton. Sometimes he'd go alone. He'd take a gun and some beers with him and reconnect with wide open American skies and freedom. He'd hunt during the day and sleep beneath the stars at night, using the time away from the non-stop hustle of the music business to press pause for a moment, to remember where he came from, reflect on where he'd been and decide where he wanted to get to. Eddie's nephew Bobby recalls one occasion which began with Eddie coming back from a hunting trip with a dead cow in the trunk of his car. The carcass was hung from the ceiling of brother Bob's garage where he then set about butchering it. When asked, brother Bob's story of how the cow came to be in his trunk involved a sorry tale of the hunters accidentally hitting the beast with brother Bob's 54 Buick Century while they were out on the road. Nephew Bobby would come to learn years later that the tale he learned as a child wasn't quite true, that the cow had died after the merry band had driven past it and Eddie had had brother Bob pull over. Eddie had then downed the cow with a .22 bullet straight through its eye, then helped load the thing into the car. Once brother Bob had finished butchering the cow he dug a hole in his back yard, buried the remains and thought nothing more of it. The neighbourhood dogs soon became interested in what was buried beneath brother Bob's garden though and began to congregate in such numbers that it soon became necessary for Eddie, brother Bob and Bob Denton to dig up what was left of the cow, load it up onto a flatbed and bury it again, this time on a secluded beach. They buried the carcass but the flatbed got stuck in the sand as they were trying to make their escape. Then the cops arrived. Some quick thinking and smooth talking ensured that the cops left them alone, but the close call left the three co-conspirators in need of a drink, so they stopped off at a few bars on the way home and toasted the cow, the cops and their own good luck. On another occasion relayed by nephew Bobby, Eddie and brother Bob did actually hit a cow with their car and load it into their trunk. Loading a cow into the trunk of a sedan is hard work, the pair of brothers were still sweating from the exertion when a few miles down the road, booming and mooing sounds started emanating from the back of the car. It didn't take the real Cochran brothers long to realise that what they actually had in the trunk was a very alive, very scared and very dangerous cow. They pulled over and choreographed their next move. One brother was going to have to pop the trunk and the other would have to open fire with Bob's Ruger semi-automatic. When Johnny Rook went out to the desert with Eddie he ended up with a beercan on his head and a drunk Eddie Cochran taking aim at it, in the dark.

Jerry Capehart stayed true to his word. He drew up a management contract and signed Sharon Sheeley to it. Sharon was now in Eddie's orbit, they were seeing more and more of each other and both were liking what they saw. Sharon was sociable and fun, she liked to throw parties so one night Eddie drove over to Sharon's place with Warren Flock. The guest list was testament to Sharon's rock'n'roll 'It' girl status, Ricky Nelson was there, The Everly Brothers were there, the exciting little crew of young Hollywood songwriters that Sharon hung out with were there. This was Sharon's turf, and Eddie was impressed. He started hanging out at Sharon's place more and more, talking music, writing songs and drinking a beer or two. Sometimes it was just the two of them, sometimes they'd be joined by other songwriters or musicians and it would get rowdy. Eventually, inevitably, Sharon and Eddie stole a moment, alone somewhere, and got together.

The teen mags loved it. Sharon and Eddie were too perfect. The up-and-coming, down-to-earth rocker and the talented and glamorous songwriter hand-in-hand in Hollywood with the world at their feet. Eddie and Sharon looked good together, Eddie with his roguish good looks and his knowing smile, cute Sharon with her teased hair and shades. The photos the teen mags ran show a close couple. Eddie raising Sharon up in the air, handing her a flower. It was getting to be for real though, the Eddie and Sharon thing, it was turning into something. Behind the magazine photos and the insider gossip and the PR machine, a genuine relationship was forming. They were teenagers and they

(Above and opposite top) The morning after the night before. Eddie keeps it together for the cameras following his big night out with Johnny Burnette.

were falling in love, just like they did in the songs. Sharon started to accompany Eddie when he went away to play more and more, hanging out with Jerry while Eddie worked.

Sharon brought out Eddie's chivalrous side. When a member of security staff in a New York hotel mistook Sharon for a prostitute and started to hustle her out of the building, Eddie decked the guy and sent him down a flight of stairs. On another occasion, when a friend they were with used the word 'motherfucker' to curse another driver, Eddie told him he should knock him flat on his ass for using language like that in front of Sharon. But Eddie was no perfect boyfriend. A movie date the pair had arranged coincided with rockabilly legend Johnny Burnette passing through town. Sharon got ready and sat waiting for Eddie to come pick her up, it was getting close to the time they had to leave to make the movie when Eddie finally called. There was a ton of traffic on the freeway he told her, but he would get there as soon as he could. Eddie wasn't stuck in traffic, nor was he making his way to Sharon's building. He was already there, in an apartment beneath hers with Johnny Burnette, a couple of hookers and a bottle or two. Once the bottle or two ran out, Johnny and Eddie came up with a plan to save both of their nights. Johnny would drive Eddie to the liquor store where they could pick up a couple more bottles. They'd return with the new stock of booze and then go their separate ways for the evening, Eddie would pick up Sharon and go see a movie, and Johnny would pick up the party with the hookers and the fresh liquor.

The plan went brilliantly until Johnny Burnette crashed his car straight into the side of a brand new Cadillac, wrote it off and got into a fight in the street with the guy driving it. The cops were called, and in the time it took them to get to the scene, Johnny and Eddie had rolled their car into a shadowy side street. The cops had no time for whatever it was Johnny thought he was doing, so they busted him there and then and hauled him off to jail. Johnny Burnette was due to appear in court the next morning so Eddie got him an attorney and showed up when Johnny was due to appear to support his fellow rocker. But Johnny was still drunk and decided to cuss out the cops who arrested him and call them bastards for half-emptying the sealed bottles of booze they'd taken as evidence when they'd eventually found his car. Eddie's day wasn't over with his visit to Johnny Burnette at the courthouse. He had a photo-shoot booked with Sharon, one of the lovey-dovey shoots with an accompanying article about their perfect romance. It was going to be tricky at best. Out-takes from the photo session tell a slightly more realistic story of the relationship between Eddie Cochran and Sharon Sheeley, Eddie arriving late and worse for wear, Sharon rolling her eyes and shaking her head, the pair then getting down to business and posing for the shots that would top that week's golden couple article about them. Eddie's protestations that the whole thing was Johnny's fault didn't wash with Sharon, she knew full well that if she'd asked Johnny whose fault the disastrous night had been, the rockabilly wildman would have pointed his finger straight at her boyfriend.

(Above) Johnny Burnette and his brother, Ray. Johnny and Ray were with Eddie when they crashed the car.

Eddie, Sharon, Sharon's sister Mary Jo and Guybo, in and around the apartment block where Sharon lived with Mary Jo at Park Sunset Apartments, 8462 Sunset Blvd, LA. These photos were part of a publicity shoot arranged by Jerry Capehart.

100

Recording Exclusively for Liberty Records. Hollywood, Calif.

EDDIE COCHRAN

Chapter Sixteen

EDDIE WAS PLAYING hard, but he was working hard too, He was using the gaps in his own fast-filling schedule to work on other people's projects every chance he got. He played on a bunch of Bob Denton recordings for Dot Records and took part in a Troyce Key session in the summer of 1958 co-produced by a young Lee Hazlewood. Time was tight at the Troyce session, they had three hours to get three songs down so Troyce explained what he wanted and Eddie gave it to him. He came up with the guitar solo for 'Watch Your Mouth' on the spot, he injected Troyce's version of 'Baby Please Don't Go' with just the right amount of sleaze and helped squeeze all of the heartbreak out of the Ray Charles tearjerker 'Drown In My Tears'. When Liberty Records founded their subsidiary label Freedom, Eddie had yet another musical outlet and more sessions to play on. The Freedom label couldn't quite bottle the lightning of Liberty's chart success with its roster of acts, but it did sign the car-crashin', cop-baitin' Johnny Burnette who, after a while on the label, moved over to Liberty. The deal was negotiated by Burnette's new manager, Jerry Capehart. Eddie's signing to Liberty hadn't stopped Jerry Capehart from digging out deals and chasing down chances. In August, he signed with Dot Records to release a couple of novelty tunes under the name Jerry Neal. 'I Hates Rabbits', the A-side of the release, may have been fun to make but didn't catch the public's imagination while the instrumental B-side, Scratchin', was a chance for Eddie to experiment and shine, which he took full advantage of. Si Waronker, while appreciating some of Jerry's input and ideas, did sometimes wonder why he was around the studio quite so much.

For their part, Liberty were now wondering how to follow up the huge success of 'Summertime Blues'. Eddie and Jerry had been working on a tune called 'Let's Get Together' that sounded right. It was infectious and driving and had enough in common with 'Summertime Blues' for it not to feel like too much of a risk. An evening session was booked on the tenth of October to record the song with Eddie, Guybo and drummer Earl Palmer joined by piano player Ray Johnson. They recorded the song but something didn't quite jive when they played it back. It was something in the phrase used as the song's title. 'Let's Get Together' just didn't scan right, so they changed it around a little and rewrote it a little and chose instead to build the song around a phrase that turned up in the first line of the lyric, 'C'Mon Everybody'. The song did ok, but not as well as expected or hoped for. It reached number thirty-five on the chart and, given the fact that everyone loved 'C'Mon Everybody' and it had a dedicated promo push behind it, it's something of a mystery as to why it didn't climb higher in the US, although the song did reach number six on the UK chart. A year previously everybody around Eddie would have been over the moon with a single at number thirty-five on the charts.

The rock'n'roll package tours still criss-crossed the country and pulled in the crowds. The bus loads of rockers hit a new town every night, gave the best show they could, had the most fun they could then got back onto the bus and tried to get some shuteye before repeating the process the next day. Eddie was becoming more confident on stage and taking advantage of the fun that life on the road had to offer. Of the stories of Eddie on the road, some are true and some are myth and some a mixture of the two. Onstage he was honing his show with the collar up on his shirt, his 6120 moving with him, working with him, getting to where it needed to be when he needed it to be there so he could slam home the riff. To let off steam after the shows they'd throw a party in someone's hotel room. Most people would bring a bottle, Eddie would bring his guitar too. Phil Everly remembers Eddie holding court on the hotel bed, playing a tune or two for the girls who joined him there. Eddie was an old hand at touring now and had a few on the road tricks up his sleeve, like carrying a bottle of booze around with him so he'd have something to pour when he offered a girl a drink. One party got a little out of hand, people just kept coming and soon the room was jammed with rock'n'roll stars and girls looking to party with them. It got rowdy, then it got raucous, then there was a banging on the door and a very angry hotel manager stepped into the room with a local cop. The party was over, the manager told the assembled guests, and anyone not staying there had to vacate his hotel pronto. The guests left in single file, each squeezing past the cop at the door to do so. Eddie was the last man out.

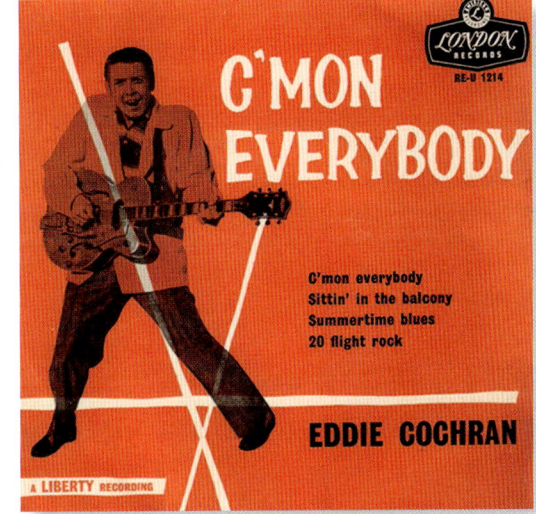

Eddie Cochran..
..Idol of the Teen-Agers

Think of a jet-propelled missile hurtling itself into the stratosphere and bursting forth in a blinding galaxy of light and you have an idea of the meteoric rise of young Eddie Cochran.

Eddie Cochran was born October 3, 1938, in Oklahoma City, Oklahoma. The youngest of five children, he is the only member of his family who has chosen the entertainment field for his profession.

Eddie began his career by singing and playing the guitar for local civic organizations and by performing at school dances, etc. After moving to California in 1953 he was soon in demand for local dances and school occasions. He also became very popular among recording artists for his ability with the guitar, and has played accompaniment for several top artists at their recording dates. As an instrumentalist, he records under the name of Kelly Green.

At a recording date he met Jerry Capehart, who convinced him to try for a recording contract on his own. This was soon accomplished when Simon Waronker of Liberty Records heard him sing and play. He was then spotlighted in the 20th Century Fox picture, "The Girl Can't Help It," and soon after was called on by Warner Bros. Studios for a leading role in their picture, "Untamed Youth."

Eddie's latest motion picture is "Go, Johnny, Go."

He has toured with all the top shows in the United States and has worked such popular clubs as the Sands Hotel in Las Vegas. He has been featured on numerous network TV shows, including the "Dick Clark American Bandstand Show."

His first recording for Liberty Records was "Sittin' in the Balcony." This was followed by "Drive-in Show." His most recent big hit was "Summertime Blues." "C'mon Everybody," backed with "Don't Ever Let Me Go." has been acclaimed an over-night smash hit, thus making Eddie a very popular young man. "Teen-Age Heaven" is another big hit by the personable recording artist.

Already four of Eddie's tunes have surpassed the million mark in sales — an unusual feat for a youngster just barely out of his teens.

He stopped in front of the cop and, unable to resist mischief, told him 'you wouldn't do this if Eddie Cochran was here.'

Eddie's final shows of 1958 were eleven straight nights at Loew's State Theatre in Times Square, New York, where Alan Freed was holding his Christmas Jubilee show. Sharon flew out with Jerry to see Eddie and catch the shows. Sharon and Eddie had been apart for a while. Their romance was thriving on the pages of the teen mags but in real life, with Eddie away so much and the particular temptations which road life offered, things were getting more complicated. The coming years would prove just how complicated things were getting, when a couple of Eddie's on-the-road dalliances ended up in paternity suits. Sharon bought a bunch of new dresses for the trip and wore the hell out of them but put on her trusty jeans to ring in the New Year, possibly inspiring the Sharon meets Eddie story as told in the '80s Levis ad.

As far as recording went, Eddie had ducked back into the studio in October of 1958 and ended what had been a tumultuous but ultimately rewarding year by getting together with Mario Roccuzzo, a songwriter he'd been writing a promising little tune with. They'd started working on the song together at actor Corey Allen's, place on Sunset Strip. Corey had been in *Rebel Without A Cause*, and while they were hanging out at his apartment Eddie had picked up his 6120 and Mario had got his first beer buzz and between them they'd communed with the gods of killer rock'n'roll and come up with 'Nervous Breakdown'. Mario came by the studio as it was being recorded and was blown away to hear the tune he'd helped write the first time he'd gotten drunk being given the Eddie Cochran treatment. All in all, 1958 ended a lot better than it had started for Eddie. He'd had a couple of big hits and had a ball touring, recording and playing with his friends, who now also happened to be some of the most famous rockers in the world.

True Romance: Eddie in a UK comic strip.

Eddie's performance of 'I Remember' in the 1959 movie *Go, Johnny, Go!* was regrettably cut from the released version and replaced by Ritchie Valens' 'Ooh, My Head!', using the same set but with three different girls seated at the table.

Chapter Seventeen

THE ORIGIN OF the phrase 'rock'n'roll' is hard to pin down. What is sure is that Alan Freed, the DJ turned concert and tour promoter, helped to popularise the term and define what it meant, how it looked and what it sounded like. Freed had hosted the *Camel Rock and Roll Party* radio show since 1956, sponsored by Camel cigarettes, which he used as a vehicle to play records by the new artists and in the process grow his own, mainly teenage, audience. Freed was an early mover in the rock'n'roll movie industry, appearing in some of its defining movies such as *Rock Around the Clock*, *Rock, Rock, Rock*, *Mister Rock and Roll*, and *Don't Knock the Rock*.

Freed's latest project was a new movie aimed squarely at the rock'n'roll audience by the name of *Johnny Melody* and Eddie began the New Year of 1959 by recording his musical contribution to the film. He then grabbed a couple of days downtime before getting back to the studio to record a couple of numbers he'd written with Jerry, including the cool breeze wish-list of 'Teenage Heaven'. The song featured a saxophone and a confidently polished, less stripped-back sound and it was agreed that it should be Eddie's next single. The tune was released in January with another song recorded at the same session, 'I Remember', on the flipside. Once again, high hopes for the song were dashed against the rocks of poor sales and a low chart position. The single only just made it into the Top 100, peaking at number ninety-nine.

By the time Alan Freed's *Johnny Melody* hit cinema screens it had been renamed *Go, Johnny, Go!* Eddie's song 'I Remember' hadn't made the final cut but a cut of 'Teenage Heaven' was still there. Eddie appears in the movie in one of the loose cardigans he was starting to favour and is preserved for posterity alongside Jackie Wilson, The Cadillacs, Ritchie Valens, who puts in a killer performance of 'Ooh My Head' and Chuck Berry, who steals the show. Chuck Berry was part of the first wave of rock'n'rollers that hit while Eddie was still peddling country and western swing with Hank and had been born Charles Edward Anderson Berry in 1926. From 1955 onwards, Chuck recorded a brace of iconic, unforgettable rock'n'roll 45s that spoke directly to the teenage audience, be they black or white. Chuck had garnered some life experience by the time the hits started, he'd spent three years in reform school for armed robbery when he and a bunch of his friends robbed three stores and stole a car at gunpoint, then he'd spent time trying to live a normal life as a married man, working on an assembly line building cars. But Chuck Berry was never destined for normal. His big break came when Muddy Waters suggested that he get in touch with Leo over at Chess Records, Chuck took Muddy's advice and recorded 'Maybellene' for the label and scored his first hit record. Following the success of the song, Chuck named his trusty guitar in its honour. Chuck knew that the show was every bit as important as the song and developed a stage act that very quickly became his trademark. Chuck would crouch low with Maybellene almost scraping the stage as he popped his neck and duckwalked from one side of it to the other, smiling that smile at the girls in the front row. Lyrically, Chuck plugged straight in to the new obsessions with hot cars and first love because he shared them. Chuck was wild and authentic and had drawn from a wide range of influences to create his unique sound. From as early as 1953, Chuck had been incorporating country tunes into his set, which mostly featured blues and R'n'B numbers. People didn't get it at first, but Chuck and his long-term collaborator Johnnie Johnson kept playing those songs until eventually his then mainly black audience caught up and started to request the hillbilly stuff. 'Maybellene' sold a million copies to black and white kids alike and Chuck had a huge crossover hit on his hands that reached the upper echelons of both the R'n'B and pop charts. When the record first appeared, Alan Freed was listed as co-writer of the tune, alongside Russ Fratto, a friend of Leonard Chess' with alleged mob connections, and Chuck wasn't happy at all. Chuck sued Alan and won, and from then on received a full credit on the tune and earned the reputation of a man with his eye on the bottom line who wouldn't let even the most insignificant detail slide. Perhaps because he was that little bit older when fame hit, Chuck wasn't prepared to give any of it away. Chuck opened his own club down in St. Louis, Chuck Berry's Club Bandstand, and furthered the cause of racial integration by declaring the club would operate an open, non-segregated door policy.

New kid on the rock'n'roll block, Ritchie Valens, was in *Go, Johnny, Go!* too, playing a 6120 just like Eddie's. Ritchie and Eddie were tight. The pair had appeared on the same package tours and would hang out together in their free time. Ritchie had been born Richard Steven Valenzuela in 1941. He'd grown up over there in the San Fernando Valley and was said to have been musical since the age of 5. He'd been so determined to learn guitar that even though he was left-handed, he learnt to play with his right. In a chilling premonition of what Ritchie's future held, when he was 15 years old, two planes collided above his high school in Pacoima. Ritchie wasn't at school that day, he was at his grandfather's funeral, but the incident did cause him to begin to have recurring nightmares and left him with a not unjustified fear of flying. Ritchie's 'La Bamba', the flipside to 'Donna', was Valens's rock'n'roll reimagining of a traditional Latin folk song and had been released two months earlier. 'La Bamba' was an instant classic. With the chart-topping success of 'Donna' and 'La Bamba', a song sung in Spanish, Valens helped to introduce and define Chicano culture and Latino rock'n'roll. Ritchie was playful, like Eddie. Live, he would improvise guitar parts during songs and change the words. Ritchie was younger than Eddie and more often than not he found that he was the youngest guy in the room. Eddie could relate.

Eddie was still on the road when time allowed in early 1959 and as always, the road was throwing up its heady array of temptations and distractions. Dexedrine and Benzedrine were the popular uppers of the day and often called upon to help get a tired musician or two's blood pumping before they hit the stage. Eddie's intoxicant of choice still took the form of the slugs he'd take from the bottle he carried around but he was no stranger to pills and their effects, and if someone needed some, then Eddie could hook it up. One time, in November of 1958, when he and Jerry were in Cincinnati for a show, they elected to book a private flight to get them to their next stop in Philadelphia. The flight was cold, cramped and uncomfortable and the wind outside was freezing. Soon the plane's instruments were icing over and at one point Jerry, who'd flown planes during the war, was up in the cockpit scraping ice from dials so the captain could see what he was doing. They made an emergency landing at a small airport but finding it closed, had to take off again. Finally, things got too scary in the air and the plane landed for good, this time in a small airfield in the midst of a snowstorm. Life on the road was unpredictable, fun and glamorous one minute, terrifying the next. At one show, Eddie pulled his gun on a dude who'd been giving him a hard time during that night's gig, at another, Eddie and the band were questioned when they were mistaken for the crew who'd just carried out an armed robbery in the town they'd just played.

NO. 3   August 3, 1959

EDDIE COCHRAN

Twenty-year-old Eddie Cochran has had four hit records on the Liberty label, but his newest release, "Teenage Heaven," is being acclaimed as the best sermon for the saddle shoe set to come along in years.

"I guess the song's power comes from the fact that it typifies the dreams of most young people," Eddie said recently in Hollywood.

"It develops the theme that in today's world, where teenagers are enveloped with the complexities of a modern society, they try to escape into a life of wonder and imagination. It's the easy life; the life of fancy cars, carefree days at the beach, soft music and moonlit nights. It's a heaven where no adults are around, where young people live their own lives within the serenity of their own thoughts."

There may be a teenage heaven somewhere in this universe of ours, but although Eddie Cochran belts out what sould become one of the biggest sellers in England, his own life tends to make the song a paradox.

For Eddie, himself, is constantly on the move. He doesn't have times for dreams these days. If he's not cutting a new record for Liberty, he's out on the road, doing personal appearances, playing before huge audiences in civic auditoriums and making the rounds of disc jockeys from coast to coast.

You could say that Eddie's in his own "Teenage Heaven" these days as the result of a number of happy occurances in Hollywood. First, the noted 20th Century-Fox producer Jerry Wald wants Eddie to sing the title song for his upcoming production to star Fabian, "Hound Dog Man." Eddie, it is understood, will also portray a featured role in the picture.

According to Wald, Eddie has all the potential for a dramatic actor and his youthful resemblence to Marlon Brando in some still pictures has stimulated the studio to give the Liberty Records' song star a screen test. It could be that the recording business may lose Eddie to motion picture, but Eddie says that music is his first love and he'll never leave it.

(over)

-2-

When Eddie reaches the age of 21, he'll embark on a new phase
of his career--that of a night club entainer. He's already
preparing his songs and arrangements, but the highlight of the
act will be a Gene Kelly-type dance. Nick Castle, one of Film-
land's top choreographers, who has worked with Jerry Lewis,
Dean Martin and other great show business names, will choreograph
Eddie's dances. Eddie will also play the drums, trumpet and
piano in the act. Two Las Vegas hotels and the Latin Quarter
in New York are now bidding for his services.

A press release for 'Teenage Heaven'.

Friday, March 20, 1959

EDDIE COCHRAN ROCKS INTO TOP 20!

VERY few people in this country outside the record-buying fraternity have ever heard of Eddie Cochran. Yet in the disc industry he has created a tremendous impact on both sides of the Atlantic. He is undoubtedly one of the names who should be noted for future international success on a large scale.

It has long been claimed, not without reason, that America is more rock-conscious than Britain. Yet, so far as young Mr. Cochran is concerned, he not only did almost as well in Britain as in the States with his first major hit, "Summertime Blues," but is now forging ahead with his follow-up release in Britain to an extent far in excess of that in America.

Last week, Eddie's recording of "C'mon Everybody" entered the NME list entries list in 20th position (this week it is in 15th place), an outstanding achievement by a young man who is virtually unknown here.

Eddie's only important showcase in Britain was in the Jayne Mansfield film, "The Girl Can't Help It", in which he performed a number called "Twenty Flight Rock" to good effect. The only trouble was that there were so many guest appearances in this movie that Eddie's solitary song tended to "get lost"!

He has subsequently appeared in a film called "Untamed Youths", which starred Mamie Van Doren, and has now just completed a picture which gives him his biggest part to date. It's called "Bop Grill" and is expected to open here shortly.

Will Eddie Cochran last? Well, first and foremost, it is this writer's opinion that, based upon the standard and appeal of his waxings to date, Eddie is no overnight sensation.

I think he's here to stay. He's already proved that he's no one-disc wonder.

His recording career began purely out of his own initiative. Out in California he met up with up-and-coming artist by the name of Jerry Capehart, who was sufficiently impressed with the youngster to recommend that he should try for a disc contract.

Jerry had been recording for the Liberty company, and he suggested that Eddie should go along and see his bosses, Si Waronker and Jack Ames. Being an ambitious artist, Eddie took the advice, and presented himself at the Liberty offices.

Hit potential

Liberty is a go-ahead concern, and they are always prepared to listen to prospective talent; they made no exception in Eddie's case. Within a matter of minutes of the audition commencing, the two executives were quick to realise that here was hit potential indeed. They signed Eddie to the dotted line as a Liberty recording artist.

He was rushed into the recording studio to cut his first sides for commercial release. Before long his waxing of "Sittin' In The Balcony" was on sale. It proved no world-shatterer by any means, although it was a moderate hit in America.

However the follow-up release boosted Eddie to world-wide acclaim. Eddie's version of "Summertime Blues" rose to No. 13 slot in the "Billboard" charts in America, while over here he climbed to 18th position.

Now, with his latest "C'mon Everybody" issue, we in this country have taken the lead and pushed Eddie into the top twenty before his own fans at home.

Eddie is only twenty years old and hails from the State of Oklahoma. He is one of a family of five children and, rather surprisingly, is the only member of the family to show any leaning towards the world of entertainment.

In demand

He began by performing at local functions around Oklahoma City and then, much to the benefit of Eddie's career, the family moved to California. He soon found himself in demand at dances and social functions, and it was at one such event that he met Jerry Capehart—and the chain of circumstances leading up to Eddie's recording contract was launched.

He has subsequently appeared at some of the nation's most important cabaret spots, and is currently engaged upon a lengthy personal appearance tour.

A thoroughly competent singer and guitarist, Eddie has more than proved his entitlement to recording success.

If he maintains the consistency which he has shown from the outset, it is more than likely that some enterprising impresario will bring him across the Atlantic to Britain in the near future.—DEREK JOHNSON.

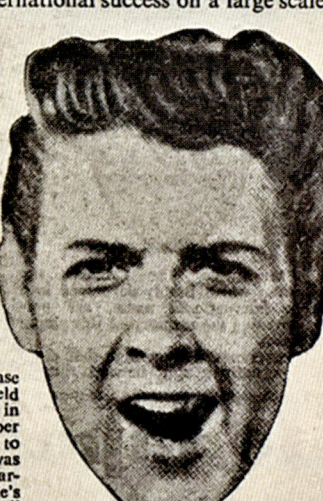

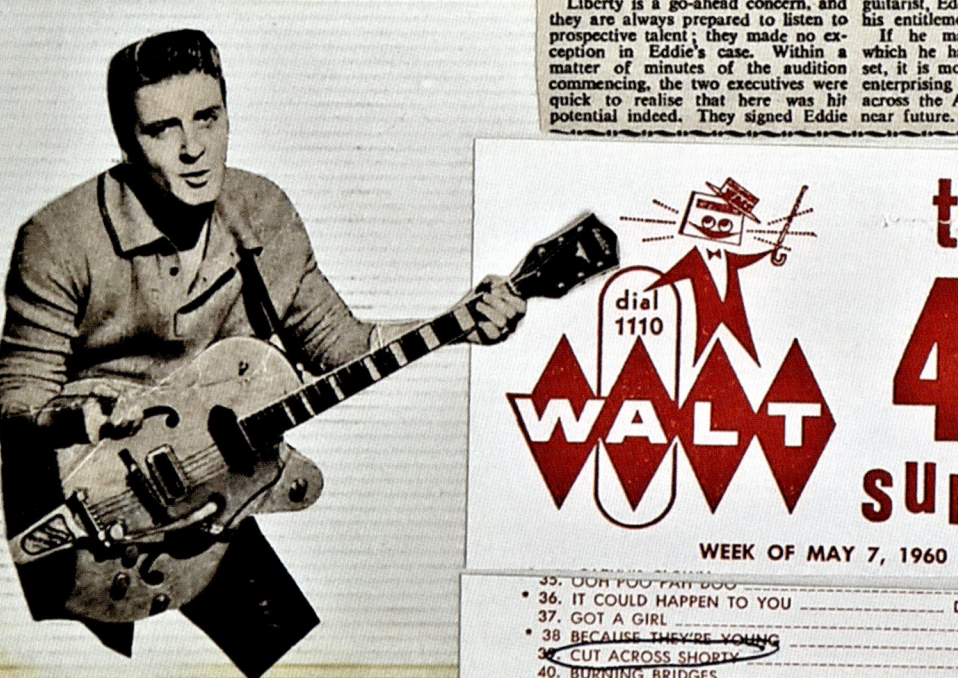

dial 1110 WALT top 40 survey
WEEK OF MAY 7, 1960

35. OOH POO PAH DOO	
36. IT COULD HAPPEN TO YOU	Dinah Washington
37. GOT A GIRL	Four Preps
38. BECAUSE THEY'RE YOUNG	Duane Eddy
39. CUT ACROSS SHORTY	Eddie Cochran
40. BURNING BRIDGES	Jack Scott

MOTION PICTURE

NOV 16 MAGAZINE

7. EDDIE COCHRAN

Eddie

"A little of Presley, lots of sexiness and a voice that, up till now, has been changing, experimenting—it all adds up to Eddie, one of the most interesting looking, acting, seeming guys in the field. Reserved, intense, he can stare you down with a look that, I'm told, makes a girl's knees go weak. One of these days, fans will discover how much fun it is to figure out Eddie's moods, decipher what's going on in his mind—in other words, get to know a boy who could make it big—suddenly! Some said he used to sound too much like Presley. But give his latest disc a spin and you'll see he sounds like Eddie Cochran—and that's a good way to be. All by himself, without help from anybody, he has that magic ingredient known as 'the excitement factor.' Keep your eyes on Eddie, he's definitely going places."

Dear Miss Winters:
   Please print this in memory of the late Eddie Cochran: Eddie was a great guy and a wonderful singer. But Fate chose to take this shy, quiet, and sincere boy away from his loved ones.

   May Eddie always be remembered and I hope and pray his *Three Steps To Heaven* are an easy climb and that his *Teenage Heaven* will be a bright and happy one.
                    Barbara Willoughby
Lockbourne, Ohio

16 MAGAZINE

THE NEW **WCOL** DIAL 1230
HITS OF THE WEEK
Columbus' Only Authentic Survey
WEEK OF MAY 16, 1960

JUST A CLOSER WALK WITH THEE	Jimmy Rodgers—Roulette	26
OUR WALTZ	Sarah Vaughn—Mercury	30
FOR LOVE	Lloyd Price—ABC Paramount	39
THREE STEPS TO HEAVEN	Eddie Cochran—Liberty	—
THATS YOU	Nat Cole—Capitol	28
SIXTEEN REASONS	Connie Stevens—Warner Bros.	25

Eddie Cochran

WYSE PIC ALBUMS
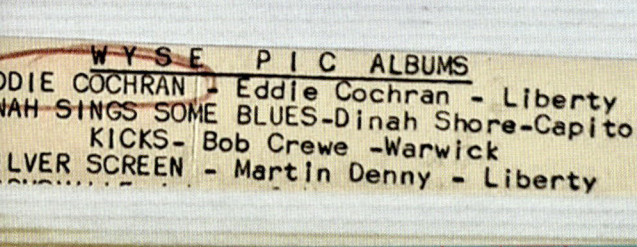
EDDIE COCHRAN — Eddie Cochran — Liberty
DINAH SINGS SOME BLUES—Dinah Shore—Capitol
KICKS—Bob Crewe—Warwick
SILVER SCREEN — Martin Denny — Liberty

Chapter Eighteen

BACK IN LA, any excitement at the upcoming theatrical release of *Go, Johnny, Go!* or the release of 'Teenage Heaven' was rendered irrelevant when, on 3 February, some awful, awful news began to spread. It sounded unbelievable at first. It sounded impossible. It couldn't be true, but it was. Just after midnight on 3 Feb 1959, Ritchie Valens, Buddy Holly and J.P. Richardson, better known by his stage-name The Big Bopper, boarded a chartered plane. They were in Clear Lake, Iowa, where they'd been taking rock'n'roll to the heartlands. But it was a rough winter that year, the heartlands were stormy and unpredictable, they were covered in snow and ice and the weather was showing no signs of letting up. The show had been on the road for eleven days but it felt way longer, they were all tired and their clothes were dirty. Despite all of their discomfort, the shows they were putting on every night were great, they were the chance for them to let out all their frustrations, crank up the amps and do their job. There was love for them out there and they were raising the roof off the joint at every single gig, but the travelling stopped being fun a few thousand miles ago and thoughts were turning to warmth, and maybe a little luxury. It was the *Winter Dance Party* tour, Buddy Holly was topping a bill that included Ritchie Valens, The Big Bopper, Dion and the Belmonts and Frankie Sardo. The *Dance Party* had started back on the 23 January, in Milwaukee, then headed out from Wisconsin to a bunch of dates in Minnesota and Iowa. For many of the towns they passed through it was like the martians had landed. The audience had seen these people in the movies and on television, they'd read about them in magazines and heard them on the radio, on the jukebox and on their own turntables at home, but here they were, in the flesh. Here was Buddy singing 'Peggy Sue', here was Ritchie cranking up 'La Bamba', here was The Big Bopper singing 'Chantilly Lace'. Despite showcasing some of the cream of rock'n'roll talent, the tour had been poorly planned, the gigs were too far apart and getting from one to another in time to jump onstage and rock meant long, cold travel days and non-stop hustle nights. Sweat and freeze, over and over. Transport on the tour came in the form of these crappy second-hand school buses, there was no heating on the buses, the ride was less than smooth and they kept breaking down. So unreliable were the old school buses that they went through five of the things in eleven days. It might not have been so bad if the tour from hell wasn't having them cover such huge distances. Many of the roads they were travelling were frozen and treacherous, the snow wouldn't stop falling and the landscape they glimpsed through iced-over windows was unending white dotted with the vehicles which had skidded off the road and been abandoned. The musicians and crew aboard the buses could see their breath, the suspension bounced them around too much, they could never get comfortable and it was all taking its toll. When things got ridiculous they'd light a fire in the aisle between the seats. So bad were conditions on the tour that Buddy's drummer, Carl Bunch, got frostbite in his toes.

By the time 2 February rode around, Buddy had had enough. He wanted off the bus for a while. He wanted to sleep in a bed and wash his clothes. Everyone wanted clean clothes. These guys took pride in their appearance, they wanted to look good and feel good but the longer they were on tour, on this tour, the harder that got. Their schedule meant that they were either on the road or at the gig, no time had been built in to do laundry, they'd been wearing the same outfits for days. Buddy wanted to fix up, to put on a fresh, clean shirt, wake up on a feather pillow. Buddy was headlining, he was a big star, one of the biggest. Buddy Holly had scored some big hits over the previous few years, both in America and the UK, and he had a new band with him to make them come alive onstage consisting of Waylon Jennings on bass, Carl Bunch on drums and Tommy Allsup on guitar. He'd released his slew of perfect rock'n'roll pop tunes and made songwriting look effortless but nothing had been handed to Buddy and he'd put in the work to get where he was. He'd supported Elvis way back in '55 and, like Eddie leaving The Cochran Brothers, he'd eschewed the sartorial and musical style of country and western, taken a risk, followed his heart and gone all in on rock'n'roll. Holly, although still only 22 years old, had the cash on hand to charter a plane to the next stop on the tour. He rounded up everybody's laundry and said he'd take it with him, that he'd have it done in time for the next gig.

Valens, Holly and the Big Bopper made their way through vicious weather to the airport where a small group of fans were waiting to wave them off. They huddled into the seats of the single engine Beachcraft Bonanza, three of the biggest rock'n'roll stars in the world, shivering together on a private plane, and waited for take-off. It didn't take long. A half hour after the show had finished they were up in the air. They made it just over 5 miles, the plane was in the air for a matter of minutes. Then it wasn't anything anymore but tragedy and wreckage. The air-crash that killed three of rock'n'roll's most important early voices was, and still is, shrouded in mystery. What we do know is that the plane hit the ground at over 170 miles per hour, that its occupants were thrown out into a snow covered field and that the plane kept on

rolling and snapping and breaking until it came to rest, tangled in a barbed wire fence.

It took ten hours to locate and reach the wreckage. Buddy, Ritchie and JP were dead when they were found and presumed to have been killed immediately upon impact. The captain, 21-year-old Roger Peterson, was dead too. Peterson's inexperience in flying through snowstorms was noted when the report came in on the crash from the Civil Aeronautics Board, and is the closest we get to an answer to the question of what really happened that night.

Rock'n'roll is tragedy and comedy, love and hate. Rock'n'roll is glitter and romance one minute and a busted heel lying in the street the next. The plane crash was a slap in the face of rock'n'roll, it was the first intrusion into what felt it might be a never-ending party. Everybody involved, from the fans to the stars, was shocked by the awful news that started to spread out of Clear Lake. Eddie took it especially badly. Hearing the news of the deaths of his contemporaries, his friends, changed something in him forever. Eddie Cochran's success had bought him membership of a very exclusive club, and now, without warning, three of its founding members were gone. The plane crash caught Eddie in a sucker punch while he was riding high, it snuck up on him and it winded him. The fantasy of rock'n'roll met the reality of a cruel universe. Shrimper was worried about Eddie, about his reaction to the crash and the black cloud that seemed to have settled over her beloved son, so she called Johnny Rook to have him come and visit. When Johnny arrived he found the Cochran household a very different place to that which he had first visited. Alice met him at the door, her eyes red from crying, and invited him in to see Eddie. It wasn't the Eddie Cochran he was used to, the sense of humour wasn't there, the optimism and the love of fun had gone and all that was left in their place was the devastating weight of grief. Eddie made Johnny

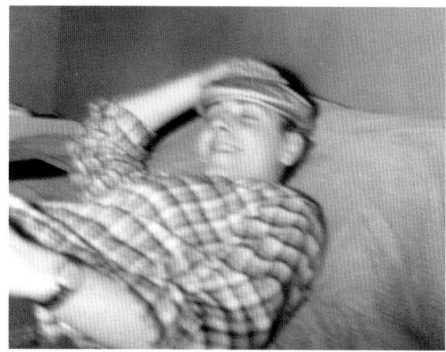

promise that if anything should ever happen to him then he would step up and keep an eye on Shrimper. Johnny said yes of course, never imagining for a moment that he might one day have to keep his promise. After a little while at the house the mood lightened somewhat, particularly when brother Bob stopped by and he and Eddie began ribbing Johnny for not playing enough Eddie Cochran tunes on his new radio show. Johnny stayed a couple of nights at Priory Street before having to return to work on the airwaves of South Dakota, there were tears and hugs before Johnny headed off to the airport and left his friend to continue coming to terms with the horrendous crash that had stolen so much talent.

Sharon Sheeley heard the news about the plane crash on the radio, just like Eddie, and was devastated. She loved Ritchie too. She'd hung out with him and Eddie in New York, he'd bought her that pair of earrings for Christmas. Eddie's reaction went beyond sadness though, it changed him, Sharon said. Forever. The news worked its way into him, into his psyche. It was the first death he'd experienced, Ritchie was even younger than he was, Buddy wasn't much older, these were Eddie's contemporaries and fellow travellers, he'd liked and admired them, now he just missed them. He'd had adventures with Ritchie, laughed with him, had fun with him. It wasn't so long ago he'd been hanging out with Ritchie Valens and Duane Eddy, eating Mexican food and drinking beer and talking music. It was unreal, yet it had happened. Buddy had scored eight hits in the US and nine in the UK before the plane crash. The Big Bopper had his second kid on the way, it was all so tragic, cruel and unfair. The ghost of that plane crash on a stormy night in February would haunt Eddie until his own dying day. It would start to visit him when he was half-drunk and alone and away from home and it would start to send him dark messages about his own fate.

(Opposite top) Eddie's 1959 Ford Country Squire outside the Cochran's new home at 10092 Bernice Circle, Buena Park CA in late 1959. Pictured with Eddie are his brother Bob and Johnnie Rook.

(Right) The day the music died.

It was too much to hold in. Eddie needed to process his grief, he needed to share his sadness and honour his lost friends. So, two nights after the crash, on 5 February, Eddie headed over to Gold Star and recorded 'Three Stars', a song about the tragedy written by Tommy Donaldson, a nineteen-year-old DJ based in San Bernadino. Eddie channelled his memories, feelings and grief into his performance of the tune at what soon became an emotionally overwhelming session for him. 'Three Stars' remembers Buddy's messy hair, the Big Bopper's Stetson hat and the fact that Ritchie was on his way to becoming something very special. The recording session for the song was traumatic, by the time they were ready to try for a fourth take of the number Eddie was inconsolable. Ritchie was seventeen. Eddie and he had gone on missions together to find Mexican food in New York. It seemed simple at the time but now all that was left were these fragmented memories of his friends and heroes, some of the memories were spectacular and some of them were mundane, but all led him straight back to Clear Lake. Recording the song was tough on Eddie, he broke down and had to leave the studio before being able to come back and finally complete his cracked, heartbroken vocal. Eddie's version of 'Three Stars' wouldn't see the light of day in the US for almost a decade, although it was released in the UK in 1966. Tommy Donaldson released his own version of the song in March of 1959 under the name Tommy Dee and scored a number eleven hit with it for Crest Records. On 7 February, Eddie appeared on the *Town Hall Party* show again and tried to heal his aching soul with rock'n'roll, playing a set that included 'Everybody', 'Money Honey' and 'Summertime Blues'. There is scant footage left of Eddie. Of that which does remain, his performance and interview at *Town Hall Party* is our best chance to see him in action and to catch a glimpse of why those who saw him perform were so bowled over. The footage is black and white of course, but the gig itself wasn't. Eddie's Gretsch flashes beneath the lights, the backing band are resplendent in matching tuxes and the joy on stage is tangible even now, sixty plus years after the event. Eddie was an experienced showman and an old hand at TV by now, and it was starting to show.

Sharon's photo which she sent to Eddie in 1959

Chapter Nineteen

AT HOME, WHEN the sessions were over and the nightclubs were closed and he was back in his room, Eddie started to sit and play the blues, looking to express the sadness of Clear Lake with his curtains drawn. Luckily for Eddie there were still lots of sessions around for him to work on, he was as in demand as he'd ever been. The work may not have taken his mind completely off the tragedy in Clear Lake, but it at least gave him something to focus on as he came to terms with what had happened. Lately, he'd begun to feel a growing resentment at the amount of tours that Jerry was booking for him and so cut down on the live work and the travel for a while, deciding to instead stay closer to home and Studio B. Touring had started to frustrate Eddie a little. In the studio he could obsess and re-record, he could reset microphones and adjust amps and change arrangements on the fly. Although Eddie loved the fans and the fun, touring too often meant making the best of it. The lack of control over his live sound wasn't working for Eddie at all so he drafted in Dick D'Agostin And The Swingers to back him on live dates. Taking his own band out with him was the more expensive option, suddenly his tour costs increased four-fold, but it was worth it. With his own, hand-picked, band behind him, Eddie had more control over his live sound and it became something they could work on over time rather than get together at soundcheck. The road life had been getting to Guybo too who, having gotten married to Marilyn, was looking to spend more time at home so he announced that he would stay in Eddie's touring band for as long as it took to find a replacement for him, but then the live stuff was out. Guybo was hard to replace, impossible really, but Eddie got it, he understood his friend's decision and didn't let it get in the way of the relationship they'd spent years building. From then on, Guybo remained Eddie's first call when lining up musicians to play on whichever studio session he might be working on. To help with his revised, more independent approach to touring, Eddie had gotten himself a new Ford station wagon, either with help from Liberty Records or his parents, which could get his band wherever they needed to be. He hitched a U-Haul trailer filled with instruments to the back of the Ford and hit the road with his very own version of The Crickets or The Blue Caps. With Guybo gone, Eddie gave Jim Stivers a shot at playing bass for him. Jim accepted and waited until they were en route to the first gig to confess to Eddie that he was a piano player and didn't know one end of a bass guitar from the other, and that he hadn't even brought one with him. Eddie was stuck and there was nothing to do but laugh and make the best of it, so in order that Jim could at least have a fighting chance while performing that night Eddie peppered the neck of a borrowed bass guitar with pieces of tape indicating where the notes were. Jim's fingers bled and he was awful, but Eddie still saw the funny side and when questioned about his bass player, announced that he was a jazz guy, hence his 'unconventional' take on the material. Eddie's backing band went through name changes and line-up iterations, they were The Swingsters, Jim Stivers and The Hollywood Swingers, and The Eddie Cochran Orchestra and the name and line-up didn't settle until Dave Shriver joined the band and they finally settled upon the name The Kelly Four.

Although their relationship was changing, Eddie and Jerry were still working well enough together to go into the studio to record a couple of instrumentals. Whatever resentments Eddie was starting to feel toward Jerry were parked while they collaborated together on the tunes 'Guybo' and 'Strollin' Guitar'. Liberty Records had worked hard to re-establish Eddie following his run of flop singles and weren't about to threaten that by releasing a pair of instrumental cuts, so the tunes were put out on American Music's subsidiary label, Silver Records. The credit on the disc goes to The Kelly Four, further distancing Eddie from the release. Another hidden Eddie recording came in the shape of the Silver release, 'Seriously In Love', credited to the Voices Of Allah. In reality the tune was written by Johnny Burnette and played by Eddie, John Ashley and The Four Dots.

Eddie was driven by the enthusiasm that had begun as a child; he loved the music, but he was also becoming increasingly aware of more adult concerns. Money was coming in and going out as Eddie became more independent and business savvy. He got a cheque book from the Golden State Bank and began using it for professional and personal expenses, sending money home when he was on the road. The star of the cheques is Eddie's signature, the fabulous, stylish curl and swoop of the E & C of his initials. The cheques illustrate Eddie's taking control of his own business and mastering his own destiny. He'd write cheques to pay bills, to help the family and treat himself to the odd piece of clothing, befitting his new standing.

Eddie was getting comfortable with his status. When he was out and about in Hollywood, he might show up at The Whip Club and join The Kelly Four, who had a residency there, for a few numbers. Eddie was making the scene and enjoying the perks his position granted him, but the music still came first. The media attention and spotlight his success shone on him was a double-edged sword for Eddie. He'd been around long enough to know that it was all a game and in order to get his music out there he had to play it, but Eddie didn't court press attention. If it came

A typical show contract from July 1959, with 50 per cent of gate receipts to be paid to the band on the night.

EDDIE COCHRAN

(back in the hit parade with 'Somethin' Else')

writes 'MY FONDEST WISH IS TO VISIT BRITAIN'

New picture of EDDIE

I GUESS my love for music dates back even further than I can remember. At least, that's what my family tells me. I am the youngest of five children. My two brothers and two sisters tell me they used to put me to sleep, when I was a baby, with the phonograph. The magic records were "Hot Pretzels" and "Beer Barrel Polka."

None of my family are in the entertainment business, but all of them have always had a love for music. They have helped and encouraged me in every way possible with my career since I first started.

I was born October 3, 1938, in Oklahoma City, Oklahoma. We moved to Albert Lea, Minnesota, while I was still a baby. I grew up there and I don't think anyone ever had a more wonderful childhood than I had.

Minnesota is a hunter's and fisherman's paradise, and my father indulged in both of these and took us along with him. That's where I get my liking for guns and hunting and all outdoor sports.

It was on one of my hunting trips that my brother shot me in the leg. We were hunting, of all things, frogs. My brother had an automatic "22" and it had refused to fire. He was trying to work the lever and it went off accidentally and shot me in the leg.

I was in bed for several months, but I still like guns, of which I have quite a few, and still go on hunting trips.

First guitar

I got my first guitar when I was ten years old. Not long after that we moved to California, and as I did not know anyone, I turned to my guitar for companionship. I really started to play in earnest then.

It was at this time I met Connie "Guybo" Smith, my bass player. We started with several more boys playing for community affairs. I remember our first paid engagement. It was for the "Town Hall" employees of South Gate, California, in the South Gate Auditorium.

I say I remember, for I was rather nervous and lost my guitar pick several times—and also my voice was just changing and it cracked several times, much to my embarrassment!

Then I heard this new music with a beat that we know as rock 'n' roll, and I knew this was for me! I started singing this music and I think it's the greatest!

It's music from the heart and that's the way I sing it. I feel it is here to stay with us maybe in a modified form, but in truth it has been with us for a long time in rhythm 'n' blues, and other forms of music.

Film break

About this time I met Jerry Capehart at a record session on which I was playing and he introduced me to Si Waronker, of Liberty Records. They arranged an audition for me and Mr. Waronker signed me to a contract.

When 20th Century-Fox asked me to appear in their picture of "The Girl Can't Help It," I got my first big break in pictures.

Soon after that Warner Brothers asked me to appear in their movie "Untamed Youth." A few months ago I just finished working in a picture for Hal Roach Studios called "Johnny Melody," which has not been released yet.

I enjoy acting very much and I hope some day to be a really great actor.

My first record release was "Sittin' In The Balcony." Much to my surprise the public liked it and even in England they seemed to like it, too.

I guess every entertainer has a dream of being able to go to England to perform, but it wasn't until my records of "Summertime Blues" and "C'mon Everybody" were released there that they asked for me.

I am so grateful to the British people for being so kind to me.

My fondest wish is to go to Britain. I planned a holiday there last summer, but I was too busy. I'll make it yet—and then I'll meet some of those kind people who have written me the best letters I've ever had.

---

to him then fine, but he wasn't actively searching it out. Eddie's ambivalence toward some aspects of the music business served him well, he was ambitious but still humble, and always ready to pop his own rock'n'roll star bubble with his self-depreciating humour and down-to-earth approach. While they were out on the road one time, Eddie told Dick D'Agostin that he was going to duck out of a radio interview he had booked, Dick was kind of shocked. Eddie should do the interview he told him, it was exposure, it'd help sell tickets and records. Eddie wasn't swayed, he had better things to do than yet another interview with yet another DJ so he sent Dick along in his place. Dick showed up and did the interview and for those twenty minutes, as far as the DJ and the audience were concerned, he was Eddie Cochran. The ruse worked and the interview was a hit. The DJ, still high from how well he'd got on with Eddie, took a couple of girls along to watch him perform that night. They arrived just in time to see Dick introduce the real Eddie Cochran, and the truth dawned.

Life on the road was ups and downs. It was beer and cigarettes, girls and guitars, late nights and long highways. They played Jack Ruby's club down in Dallas where the audience was as likely to contain members of law enforcement as it was Mafia bagmen. Extremely enthusiastic fans, the Okie Chicks, started following them from gig to gig, half a dozen girls who'd show up wherever they were playing looking to party with the boys in the band. Eddie and The Kelly Four covered the distance between gigs by flooring the station wagon and racing from venue to venue, often arriving just in time to set up and play. Eddie would bring his guns along to pass the time, he'd shoot at rabbits out of the car window or challenge people to clap their hands before he could draw his pistol. Eddie was a fast draw, most people lost that one.

According to the teen mags and the gossip hounds, Eddie and Sharon were now officially a thing, they were dating and in love and all was well, but Sharon knew the business as well as Eddie, and although he wasn't taking up all of the offers that came his way on the road, he wasn't refusing all of them either. Their time apart was causing a strain on their relationship, as evidenced by one of Sharon's letters.

Dear Eddie,

whats happening to us. we seem to be drifting further apart instead of closer together. one minute were in love the next minute were tearing each other down. I'm afraid if we keep going one day very soon we'll wake up and find our love has died. maybe its because were forced apart so much. everytime you come I feel like were almost strangers and we have to get to know each other all over again. But we never quite seem the same. Everytime we seem a little farther apart. Instead of saying things we really want to say. we play games with each other like "guess what I'm gonna do next" or "how much do you really think I love you." and we always end up hurting each other. are you sure Eddie your really are in love. Its a powerful word somtimes used to express things that arn't really true love. I want you to be sure honey because if your not I want you to have your freedom for awhile and

Dear Eddie,

What's happening to us? We seem to be drifting further apart instead of closer together. One minute we're in love, the next minute we're tearing each other down. I'm afraid if we keep going one day very soon we'll wake up and find our love has died. Maybe it's because we're forced apart as much. Every time you come back I feel like we're almost strangers, we have to get to know each other all over again but we never quite seem the same. Every time we seem a little further apart. Instead of saying things we really want to say we play games with each other like 'guess what I'm gonna do next' or 'how much do you really think I love you?' and we always end up hurting each other.

Are you sure Eddie, you really are in love? It's a powerful word sometimes used to express things that ain't really true love. I want you to be sure honey, because if you're not I want you to have your freedom, for a while, and see how things work out. The last night you were home I acted terrible three quarters of the night and I feel very bad about it. I was trying to hurt you because you were leaving me again and I had the feeling you were glad to go. Maybe you love me, but you don't need me darling.

Bob told me something the other night I'll never forget. He said 'Don't forget baby Eddie's first love in life is his music and friends.'

Sometimes I think we're both afraid of love and that's why we hurt each other.

I had to write this letter because if you feel different about things than you used to I want to break up for a while. I'm afraid you do, but you don't wanna hurt me.

Please call me when you're done reading this if you're sure. If you're not don't call, and I'll understand darling. I'm sending you the picture you asked for a long time ago. It's not as good but it's all I've got.

Love Sharon.

At the Assumption Arena in Chadron on 3 October 1959, which was also Eddie's 21st birthday.

Chapter Twenty

AT HOME, WORK-WISE, Eddie was on a roll and the recording sessions where he concentrated on material for his own career produced some killers. On 23 April 1959, he recorded 'Weekend' at United Recorders and stamped his identity all over the song which was originally written by Bill and Doree Post. When not working on his own material he did a bunch more Freedom sessions, playing on recordings by Barry Martin and Jay Johnson, and also found time to help out his friend Baker Knight on a session where they cut 'Just Relax', held up by Eddie aficionados as one of his finest rock'n'roll session performances. A session in June produced the first attempt at a song Eddie had written with Brother Bob called 'Three Steps To Heaven'. The song was good, but not yet great. A couple of changes needed to be made. The opening line wasn't scanning and needed work. When it was replaced, the whole song fell into place and a classic was born. There's a seasoned maturity in the lyric of 'Three Steps To Heaven' that belies Eddie's tender age. Although the song deals with the standard boy-meets-girl theme, it does so while acknowledging that life isn't simple or easy and that there will be bad times as well as good. Eddie Cochran was growing up.

As always, there was concern over at Liberty Records over what song Eddie should release next. 'Weekend' sounded good and so, when it was reworked, did 'Three Steps To Heaven', but those were eschewed in favour of a new tune, one that would gain Sharon a songwriting credit on an Eddie Cochran 45 and lay down a blueprint for punk rock just as many of that movement's stars and anti-stars were being born.

'Somethin' Else' is a defining moment in rock'n'roll history. The tune started life as a piece Sharon was working on with Eddie's brother Bob, with whom she shared the writing credit, although Jerry Capehart would later claim that he and Eddie had a big influence on the tune as it was being recorded at Gold Star on 23 June. The song was backed with 'Boll Weevil', a take on a traditional tune where Eddie, ever conscious of the importance and power of the myth, once again confused the story of his own origins by claiming to be from Oklahoma. The 'Somethin' Else' release earned Eddie another spot on Dick Clark's American Bandstand, and without wishing to jinx the tune and tempt fate, expectations and the promo budget were high. The single didn't do as well as it should have. It peaked at number fifty-eight on the chart but once again, the song's reception at the time of its release would come to fade from memory, while the song itself was utterly unforgettable.

There were other songs Eddie wanted to get down too, another side of himself that he wanted to express. Eddie had loved the blues since he'd heard them. When he'd been with Gene and The Blue Caps over at Capitol, the backing vocals he'd added to songs like 'Git It' had been directly inspired by the R'n'B and blues numbers he loved so much but ever since the tragedy at Clear Lake, he'd started living the blues for real. Eddie wasn't trying on the blues like you'd try on a jacket, he understood the form, he knew that doing it properly was about more than just playing the right notes in the right order, it was about feel and emotion, it was about letting the broken parts of your heart play the guitar and sing for you. Eddie had known loss now and had inherited a melancholy that would never leave him, and it came out when he played the blues. B.B. King would later say that of everybody who was dipping into the blues at the time, Eddie was the only guy who really got it. B.B. had hung out with Eddie on Lowell Fulson's front porch in LA where the three of them had jammed together, keeping the beat by tapping their feet on the wooden floor. On 25 August 1959, Eddie booked a session at Gold Star and used some of it to record his take on the blues. He got 'Eddie's Blues' down, as well as 'Chicken Shot Blues' and 'Milk Cow Blues', and illustrated perfectly why guys like B.B. King rated and respected him so much. It was a busy session. As well as the blues numbers, they finished 'Guybo' and recorded three other songs with singer/songwriter Darry Weaver. The session got a little fractious, particularly between Eddie and Jerry. Jerry wanted all the songs recorded as quickly as possible but Eddie and the band weren't quite up to speed

Eddie on stage with the Kelly Four; at the Moonlite Gardens in Wichita on the left and the City Auditorium in Hot Springs on the right.

on them, there hadn't been enough rehearsals and people weren't sure where they were supposed to come in. They were fluffing the intros and trying Jerry's patience, so when Eddie then did it on purpose and the band cracked up and another take was lost, Capehart was not amused.

They got what they needed from the session though and Eddie was back the next morning, this time to record 'Strollin' Guitar'. On 29 August, they cut 'My Love To Remember', 'Little Angel' and 'Instrumental Blues'. Now on a roll, Eddie went back to Gold Star again on 31 August to record a louche, bluesy version of Ray Charles' 'Hallejulah I Love Her So'. The recording turned out so well that it was scheduled to become Eddie's next single for Liberty. Since financial disaster had been averted and Liberty Records had got back on its feet, Si Waronker had been taking on new staff. One of his hires was an A&R guy with producer aspirations, Snuff Garrett. Snuff had produced Johnny Burnette's first single for Liberty, 'Settin' The Woods On Fire', and had his own, very strong, ideas about how a hit record sounded. So convinced was Snuff of his ability to create a chart-bound sound that, on 23 October Snuff took Eddie's master of 'Hallelujah I Love Her So' and overdubbed it with masses of orchestral violins. He then turned his attention to 'Little Angel' and added a gospel backing vocal. Eddie was, naturally, outraged, and went off at both Liberty Records and Garrett himself for taking such a, well, such a liberty.

Snuff's layers of extra production didn't have anything like the result he expected and 'Hallelujah I Love Her So', backed with 'Little Angel', failed to chart in the US. Across the Atlantic, though, over in the UK, the single did well, it hit the charts on two separate occasions and peaked at number twenty-two. Eddie had been selling well in the UK for a while, singles that weren't doing so well at home were regularly hitting the British charts.

There was a lot of love for Eddie in the UK, the support there seemed pretty unwavering and reliable and even though his British fans had never seen him in person, they had remained loyal. The thirst for rock'n'roll over in the UK was quenched to a certain extent by the home-grown acts whose entire schtick was built around their take on authentic American rockers. UK audiences had gotten to see their American idols up close when they'd toured there, playing to fans every bit as enthusiastic and wild as they were back home. Bill Haley toured the UK, so did The Platters, Buddy Holly and Frankie Lymon & The Teenagers amongst others. More and more the British charts were featuring numbers by good looking young boys with names like Wilde and Fury, guys with a curl in their lip and their collars flicked up. The Brits were utterly sold on the vision of Americana that Eddie so beautifully represented, from his birth beneath the wide open skies of Minnesota to his background in country, his love of the blues and his rock'n'roll flair. The iconic silhouette Eddie had established in *The Girl Can't Help It*, the loose young rocker with the hot guitar, the kid from the sticks with fire at his fingertips, had struck a deep chord with Britain's own brand of teenagers.

In August, Eddie was booked to perform on Johnny Otis's live TV show. Eddie swung by his buddy Ronnie Ennis's place on the way to see if Ronnie wanted to come with him and hang out and watch the show being recorded. Ronnie said he couldn't make it but that he'd watch Eddie's performance for sure when the show went out at six o' clock that evening. So Ronnie sat and watched, but when the show went out, there was no Eddie. When Eddie had eventually arrived at the studio, the taping was underway and someone decided to give him a hard time for turning up late. They picked the wrong day to yell at Eddie, who was no longer the new kid on the block, eager and grateful for every chance that came his way, but instead now a seasoned professional with a sense of

'Milk Cow Blues'. Recorded at Gold Star.

his own worth and not someone who would be dressed down by a TV producer. So Eddie turned on his heels and walked, and was back at Ronnie's place laughing about the son of a bitch who'd cussed him out before the show had ended. Eddie liked the trappings of success, he liked being a hip Hollywood kid around town, he liked that heads turned when he walked into a nightclub and that he was achieving his dreams of success, but he didn't like being treated like a kid. He was starting to rethink his career a little, to take a little more control and the only person who could tell him off was Shrimper.

Eddie's new Ford station wagon gave him way more control over where he played, when he played and who he played with, but it didn't guarantee that gigs would go smoothly. Whilst he was in the badlands of North Dakota with The Kelly Four, the band were battling through the rain that was turning everything around them into a muddy swamp. The station wagon got stuck in the mud and Eddie Cochran and The Kelly Four got covered in the stuff as they tried to heave the car and trailer out of the mire and back on to the road. Eventually a truck came by and pulled them out, but they'd been stuck a long time and by the time they got to the gig, at 11.45 p.m., there was fifteen minutes of stage-time left before the place shut down. The band were a mess, they were covered head to toe in the wet mud they'd been slipping around in as they tried to move the station wagon when they played their ten minute set to the remaining audience before the clock struck midnight.

On that 3 October 1959, Eddie Cochran turned 21 years old, having already experienced more than most do in a lifetime. At a gig in Chadron, the local radio station, KOBH, presented him with a huge cake and awarded him a trophy declaring him 'The Number One Singer in the Seven-State Area'. Johnny Rook had flown in to wish his friend happy birthday and noted how Eddie's spirits had lifted somewhat since the last time he'd seen him in the aftermath of Clear Lake. Eddie's attitude seemed to be changing. The two made plans together, deciding that Johnny should move his radio show to a bigger station and play Eddie's tunes to a larger audience. Eddie told Johnny about a tour he had coming up in England, how he was going to change his image there somewhat and dress in leather for the shows and if he was feeling especially daring, wear nothing underneath it. Photos taken later that evening show Eddie celebrating his birthday in an intimate moment with a cute girl, as The Kelly Four crowd around the would-be young lovers.

Alongside his touring schedule, Eddie had another TV appearance booked, on Dick Clark's *Saturday Night Beech-Nut Show* on 10 October where he joined the Isley Brothers and the Fireflies and performed the song that had given him his first hit, 'Sittin' In The Balcony'. All in all, Eddie ended 1959 doing what Eddie did, recording as much as possible and chasing down his dream. He got a bunch more tracks down at Gold Star and hit the Midwest with The Kelly Four. Since he'd bought the Ford pick-up touring had become easier, he could book one-off dates on his own now without having to sign up to weeks and weeks of multi-artist roadshows. His relationship with Jerry Capehart had changed too. What started as a low-stakes musical partnership had become professional. There was money involved

In the back of Eddie's 1959 Ford Country Squire, somewhere in the Midwest in October 1959.

now and Jerry's decisions had started to feel less those of a friend and more those of a stakeholder. Plus, he was distracted so much of the time now with his other clients. Jerry had signed a bunch of acts, he'd negotiated a bunch of deals and written a bunch of songs but his biggest star, and therefore his biggest earner, was still Eddie Cochran. Si Waronker had been looking askance at Jerry for a while, so when Eddie came to him and started expressing his dissatisfaction with his manager / agent / songwriting partner, saying that he was claiming songwriting credits that he hadn't earned, it didn't come as any great shock. But there wasn't an awful lot Si could do, the arrangements between his artists and their management were their own affair and far beyond the purview of a label boss. Eddie was starting to realise, perhaps a little too late, that songwriting credits were where the long term money was, that songs had a life beyond their initial release and sales figures, and he was starting to think that he may have given far too much away already. Si Waronker wasn't the only person in Eddie's circle who harboured doubts about Jerry's involvement in his career. Bob Denton wasn't convinced either and thought that although Jerry knew his way around a tune, rather than helping Eddie, Jerry Capehart was holding him back. For his part, Jerry may have been finding himself out of his depth somewhat. Despite the image he'd always projected of musical insider and industry mover and shaker, Jerry, via his connection to Eddie, was now playing in the big leagues and struggling to keep up. As Christmas approached, the gulf between them had widened to the extent that Eddie was booking his own tours, like the big one he'd lined up in England with Gene that he'd talked to Johnny Rook about, and he was now regularly recording without Jerry.

Eddie and Jerry had originally bonded when they became studio buddies, experimenting and exploring possibilities whenever circumstance allowed. Tracks like 'Guybo' allowed them to geek out, to spend as much time as it took to have the studio recreate the sounds they heard in their heads. The pair, who had been through so much together, were now very different people to when they had first met, at least Eddie was. Over the previous year he'd taken control of how, when and where he played live and what and when he recorded. He'd been forced to grow up by the death of his friends in Clear Lake and watched the public's musical taste evolve, sometimes with him, sometimes without. He was still Eddie fucking Cochran though. He was still fizzing with potential and hope, still in search of the perfect song, and still on the path toward his dream.

Throughout all of his musical career thus far, Eddie had shared his thrills and his disappointments with his family. Alice was still his rock, his North Star, Shrimper was still able to make her youngest boy's good days great and his bad days better. Over the rollercoaster ride of the last five years, Shrimper had always been there, reminding him that upsets come and go, that he was young and special and loved and that he had his whole life ahead of him. Alice and Frank were still living on Priory Street, still watching TV in the living room where Eddie and Guybo had sat for hours together learning old tunes and trying to write new ones. It was time for the Cochrans to move up in the world, they left Priory Street behind and headed to a fancy neighbourhood in Buena Park, Orange County. Sister Gloria was living at home with her husband Red and Eddie's nephew, Ed. Eddie and Ed played together whenever Eddie was back at home, Eddie got the chance to revisit cowboys and Indians with his new nephew and would hide in wait for him to start playing in his sandbox before opening fire and drenching him with a water pistol.

As 1959 turned into 1960, Eddie returned to Gold Star on 8 January for a session which resulted in recordings of 'Cut Across Shorty', 'Cherished Memories' and 'Three Steps to Heaven'. 'Cherished Memories' was one of Sharon's songs, and while Eddie was recording it at Gold Star, Shrimper was at home, packing her son's suitcases. Eddie was going on a trip.

The number one singer as voted by the listeners of KOBH Radio in Chadron Nebraska on 3 October 1959. Left to right: Mike Henderson (sax), Johnnie Rook, Eddie and Dave Shriver (bass).

April 7, 1959

Mrs. Cochran,
    I am writting you to ask if Eddie has a record that I can't find because its out of stock. It's Merle Travis's record of Cannon Ball rag.
I know Eddie use to play that style so I thought maybe by chance he had it.
If so I would like to tape it.
We are former friends of Dick Lewis and he taught my daughter to play Merle's style.
She was on Town Hall party Talent time the week before Eddie was a guest down there. She played Cannon Ball rag but later we was told she is leaving

August 6, 1959

Dear Eddie,

Hee, I'm really sorry I haven't written before, but it seems I'm always doing something or going some place.

I just wanted to write and say your record, "Somethin' Else", is real great! We'll help all we possibly can. Is there anything we should know in the way of records or movies?

I was reading a magazine and it mentioned you and Shari Sheely. All of us hope you're happy now & will be happy. I hope you don't mind my mentioning it.

Let me know if there's anything we should watch for or know about. In the future I'll try to do a better job of keeping in touch. Keep up the good work & the best of luck.

Sincerely yours, A faithful fan always,
Anna DeLence

P.S. Almost forgot, when will you be out our way again?

Chapter Twenty-one

ON SUNDAY, 10 JANUARY 1960, Pan Am 100, an international flight from California touched down in London. On board, bleary-eyed passengers began to unbuckle seatbelts, stretch their legs, reach for their hand luggage and summon the energy to get through customs and embark on the next leg of their journey. One of the passengers was especially relieved to have landed, to be back on solid ground and not have the constant voice in his head telling him that this is how his friends died. He'd been in the air for hours, suspended over the deep Atlantic Ocean with little to do but fear the flight and see the faces of Ritchie Valens, Buddy Holly and The Big Bopper every time he closed his eyes.

In the America our passenger had just left behind his beloved rock'n'roll wasn't dying, but it was changing again. There was a concerted effort within the entertainment industry to blunt its edge, the charts were starting to fill with syrup sung by dreamboats and the original wave of rockers weren't pulling in the crowds or selling the records like they had been just two years previously. Elvis was full Hollywood now, the prescription pills were starting to show as his dream of being a serious actor like James Dean crashed and burned in the face of yet another cookie-cutter script and a soundtrack deal. Little Richard had been preaching the word of the Lord since Australia and Jerry Lee, well, the ruckus about his marriage to his 13-year old cousin Myra Gale hadn't played well anywhere and the hits were drying up. Jerry Lee was pissed at the world and there was a gun nearby. Chuck Berry had gone and got himself in trouble too. He was up on charges of statutory rape, the claim being that he transported Apache waitress Janice Escalante across state lines in order to run the hatcheck concession at his club. Once there, Chuck was alleged to have had unlawful physical relations with her. Janice was 14 years old. For the dumb-fuck racists and the rock'n'roll haters, Jerry Lee's fall from grace and Berry's arrest confirmed what they'd been thinking, saying and preaching for the last four years, that rock'n'roll was an unholy meeting place for degenerates and recidivists, that nothing good would come of it and that you wouldn't catch that nice boy-next-door type Fabian kidnapping underage girls and raping them. There were a lot of Fabians around in 1960, lots of malleable, unthreatening heart-throbs singing saccharine odes to boring girls. The bottom line was that this seemingly never-ending hit parade of teen-idols were less of a risk than your Jerry Lees and your Chucks. They did what they were told, they wore what they were told and they sang what they were told to. They were rock'n'roll stripped of all its vitality, sex and danger, they were wholesome fun for the whole God-fearing family, pale imitations of what had gone before and as much fun as watching paint dry.

The flight Eddie was on, the plane touching down in London, had been long, but the good news was that it would be the last plane he'd have to board for a while as he'd be doing all of his travelling on buses and trains for the coming months. More good news was that the British tour was already a roaring success before it had even begun. Tickets were selling hand over fist and more dates were being added all the time. Amongst other names, it got called *The Fast Moving Beat Show*. It was Gene Vincent and Eddie Cochran co-headlining and backed by a band made up of the cream of British rockers as they played a string of venues the length and breadth of the UK. British kids had been thirsting for rock'n'roll since they first heard it, they'd waited years and thanks to Larry and his TV producer friend Jack, here it was. They liked the grittier stuff in Britain, they liked the rockabilly instrumental breaks and the wild abandon of all out rock'n'roll and *The Fast Moving Beat Show* was going to give it to them. The tour was the brainchild of Jack Good and Larry Parnes, the archetypal Svengali and mover and shaker who'd spent the last few years developing homegrown talent to fill the demand created by American rock'n'roll stars. For Gene, the tour was a chance to get away from America for a while where he was getting a bad reputation as truculent, unpredictable and temperamental. Gene's last manager had split, he either got fired or he quit, and the new guy at the helm of Vincent's career, Norm Riley, saw the UK tour as a way to get Gene away from the US for a while, to put him in front of some appreciative audiences and try to take his mind off the fact that his star was fading somewhat at home. Gene could still be polite, charming and attentive when he needed to turn it on but when he drank a few drinks, downed a few pain pills and let his demons run the show for a while, mean Gene came out to play. By late '59, when Gene arrived in the UK, his reputation as being difficult to work with back at home was growing, so when he first got to there he charmed people with his deference and politeness, but dark, mean Gene was always waiting at the bottom of a bottle. For Eddie, the tour was a big chance. Gene might have been regarded as the star of the show but in truth it was Eddie who was on the up. Eddie was still writing classics, he was still moving into the future while his buddy Gene was rapidly becoming defined by his past. The audience in the UK were ready for Eddie, he had fans there from way back who'd remained loyal from day one. Even the releases that didn't sell so well Stateside did well in Britain and Eddie was keen to get in front of the fans there, to thank them for their support and show them, night after night, why he warranted it. The tour was good business too and came with a decent payday for Eddie. Thanks to the exchange rate working in his favour he was getting a thousand dollars a week. His buddy Gene Vincent, the 'star' of the show, was getting more. Gene had been in the UK since before Christmas and had played a bunch of shows on his own which had gone down a storm. He was the original US signing for the tour and the initial thought was that he would headline on his own, backed by British musicians and supported by local acts. Eddie was added to the bill later, when it was thought that another American rocker with a repertoire of crowd-pleasers would push the *Fast Moving Beat Show* over the edge.

There were fans and press waiting for Eddie as he disembarked and made his way through customs. Gene was there too, with Brit rocker Billy Fury and Larry, the man who put the whole travelling beat show together. Larry was famed impresario Larry Parnes, who'd been in the business since he fell into it when he got asked to invest in some stage clothes and a decent guitar for Bermondsey boy and star in the making, Tommy Steele. Steele was Parnes's first big act and his entree into the world of British rock'n'roll, but Tommy went from rocker to family entertainer, and the kids wanted rockers. His next signings, Marty Wilde and Billy Fury, were much closer to the mark. Larry did a number on the acts he signed, as he oversaw their image and their output and even changed their names, and he was getting pretty good at it. Parnes's aesthetics where his performers were concerned were dictated by his own tastes, his boys dressed the part and there was an edge of danger there, just behind the smouldering good looks.

'The next morning, Eddie met the press again at Decca Records in London, told them about how his girlfriend may come join him on tour and smiled as he spoke about Sharon. He didn't tell them about the fight he and Sharon had before he left. He told the assembled journalists how pleased he was to be working with Gene again and he made sure to mention 'Hallelujah I Love Her So' in order to drum up a few sales. Eddie was Eddie as he spoke to the press, he was charming, funny and personable, somehow still humble yet definitely enjoying being a star.

Parnes's schedule was tight. On Tuesday 12 and Wednesday 13, Eddie had to rehearse for two TV appearances he had lined up. The show he was appearing on was called *Boy Meets Girls*, Parnes's guy Marty Wilde hosted the show with the Vernons Girls, and Eddie's performances would be broadcast over the next two episodes. Then there was yet more press for Eddie to meet, this time at a buffet at Selby's restaurant in Mayfair. Eddie showed up dressed in a leather jacket, hinting at things to come.

On the morning of 14 January, Eddie was en route to Manchester. He was there to spend a couple of days at Granada Studios taping the episodes of *Boy Meets Girls* that would be aired over the coming two weeks. The show was produced by Jack Good, and Jack liked Eddie. He liked that Eddie always knew where the camera was and what it wanted. He liked that Eddie took direction well and that he was different somehow from the other rockers and wanted to do everything he could to put on a good show for the folks at home. For their part, the folks at home didn't have a lot of viewing choice where TV was concerned in Britain in 1960. They had just two channels to pick from, both of which broadcast rock'n'roll shows that went head to head on Saturday evenings at six thirty. Jack Good's performance based *Boy Meets Girls* went up against *Juke Box Jury*, where a panel of music stars and experts listened to the latest releases and decided whether the tune in question was a hit or a miss. Twenty-nine-year-old Good had been making TV sympathetic to the new music and the culture that went with it since he started the *6.5 Special* show back in 1957. He'd then followed that show up with another music based hit, 'Oh Boy!' Jack filled his new show with the new wave of British rockers, artists like Cliff Richard and Vince Taylor would appear to give their take on what was happening in the US. When 'Oh Boy!' ended, Jack got Larry's boy Marty Wilde and The Vernons Girls on board, and *Boy Meets Girls* was born. Eddie pulled out the big guns at Granada and taped performances of 'Twenty Flight Rock', 'Somethin' Else' and 'C'Mon Everybody' in his leather pants and a loose jacket. Eddie had started wearing his brown leather jacket around too, pulling up its fur collar against the cold he was starting to feel, the damp cold that was clinging to him and turning to steam when he got inside. The leather look was no accident, Jack Good had done it on purpose. He and Larry Parnes were selling the dangerous side of rock'n'roll, the unbridled elemental wildness of it. They were selling bad boys and rebels and they wanted them to appear threatening rather than safe, they wanted them to make a statement before they'd even played a single note. Gene was in leather too, he was wearing a black leather jacket and black leather pants and had a medallion swinging at his neck, he was dragging his leg across the floor, hanging onto the mic stand for dear life, channelling the broken majesty of Richard III and inventing Shakespearean rock'n'roll.

The TV tapings were finished. Jack was happy, the studio audience loved it and even the TV crew were impressed. It was 16 January and Eddie was on his way back to London, to the flat he and Gene were staying at in Jermyn Street. He was due to start a couple of days rehearsals in Soho with the band that would be backing him for the tour, he was excited to start the rehearsals but he was nervous too. The band he and Gene were using was made up of The Wildcats, Marty Wilde's backing band, and The Beat Boys, with Georgie Fame on keys. Vince Eager's backing band would also be playing behind the American stars as well as members of the skiffle band, The Blue Flames. The rehearsals started and even though he was thousands of miles from California, Eddie soon began to feel at home. The assembled British musicians were already die-hard fans of Americana, of country and the blues, of cowboys and rebels, and here was the real thing in front of them, and he'd bought the sound they loved so much with him. He blew the assembled musicians away with his technical ability and genuine feel for the 6120. Eddie's Gretsch was one of the first seen on English shores, it seemed bigger all of a sudden, brighter, more beautifully made. He played some Chet Atkins and jaws dropped and when he played a killer intro to 'What'd I Say', he sealed the deal. Any doubts about compatibility and making the whole thing work faded pretty early in the session. The British musicians were good, they were really good, and what they didn't know already they were eager to learn. Eddie showed them finger-picking on his Gretsch and note-

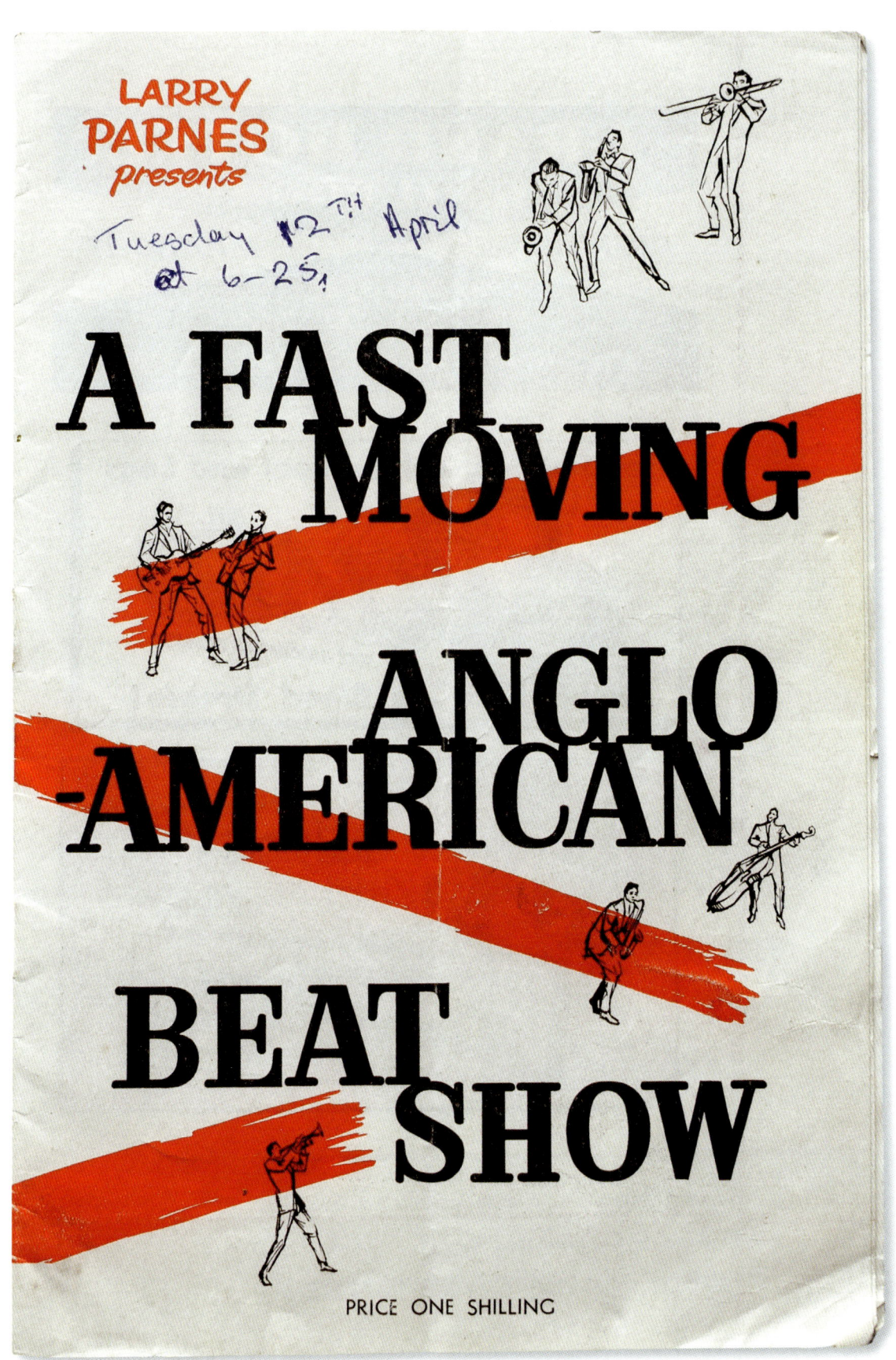

The programme for the Bristol Hippodrome from 11 to 16 April 1960, the last week of shows that Eddie played.

PROGRAMME

1. **TONY SHERIDAN GROUP**
   From T.V.'s "Oh Boy"

2. **THE VISCOUNTS**
   Britain's Newest Vocal Group

   For the first time ever in England
3. **EDDIE COCHRAN**
   Hit recorder of "Summertime Blues" & "C'mon Everybody"

   Star of T.V., Radio, Stage and Records
4. **VINCE EAGER**
   and The Quiet Three

5. **INTERVAL**

6. **BILLY RAYMOND**
   Your host and compere

7. **THE VISCOUNTS**
   Pye Recording Artistes

   The Rock 'n' Roll Idol of Millions
8. **GENE VINCENT**
   BACKED BY THE FABULOUS 'WILDCATS'
   (By kind permission of Marty Wilde)

God Save The Queen

This Programme is subject to alteration at the discretion of the Management

(Above) Programme for the One-Nighter shows on Eddie's 1960 UK tour, which started at the Ipswich Gaumont on 24 January 1960.

(Opposite) At the Hippodrome in Ardwick from 28 March to 2 April. It was during this particular week that Sharon Sheeley arrived in the UK and joined Eddie in Manchester.

bending on thinner strings. He taught drummer Brian Bennett a few tricks he'd picked up from Earl Palmer and pretty soon everyone in the room felt lucky to be there and the band started sounding great.

On 24 January, the night after Eddie's second *Boy Meets Girls* episode aired, he was in Ipswich. It was first night of the tour, what they hadn't nailed down in rehearsals they'd have to work out on stage, but Eddie was feeling good. Ipswich was a one-nighter, the tour had been divided up between them and week-long residencies and the shows were choreographed depending on where they were playing and for how long. They were doing the usual couple of shows in Ipswich, one at 6 p.m. and one and 8.30 p.m. The shows lasted a couple of hours in total so there was time for a reset between the first and second performances. Each of those performances was split into two halves with Eddie in the first and Gene in the second. When Gene and Eddie weren't on stage the home-grown rockers like Vince Eager, Billy Fury and Tony Sheridan were. Eddie was on good form as the tour opened and he met his British fans for the first time. They went crazy for him and he, in turn, went into a hip-shaking, gyrating Elvis routine when he hit the stage and told the delighted crowd how great it was to be with them here in 'Hipswich'. Eddie caught Vince Eager's act, he stood at the side of the stage and listened to Vince's take of 'It's Only Make Believe' and made sure to tell him after the show how much he dug it. Someone shouted something up at Gene during his act and Gene stopped the number and put the evil eye on the guy and told him, 'I don't know what it is that makes you tick. But I sure hope it's a bomb.' After the gig Eddie did a taped radio interview, he was coming down from the show with nowhere to go and he told the interviewer he just wanted to get some sleep.

Ipswich was the first British crowd Eddie played to so it was the first time he got to see with his own eyes how the British working class kids had adopted rock'n'roll and turned it into a lifestyle. There were Teddy Boys in the audience in long drape jackets and drainpipe pants. They were wearing crepe soled shoes and waistcoats and constantly attending to slicked back greased-up pompadours with metal toothed combs. There were rockers out there too, ton-up motorcycle kids who wanted their bikes fast and their rock'n'roll loud. And then, of course, there were the girls.

(Right) The programme and a ticket for the *NME* Poll Winners Concert at the Empire Pool, Wembley on 21 February 1960. Eddie and Gene guested amongst a star-studded cast of Britain's top music stars: Cliff Richard, Lonnie Donegan, Craig Douglas, John Barry, Billy Fury, Alma Cogan and more. Both Eddie and Gene put on storming shows after surviving an all-out riot at their gig the previous night in Dundee and then enduring a gruelling overnight train journey from Dundee to London.

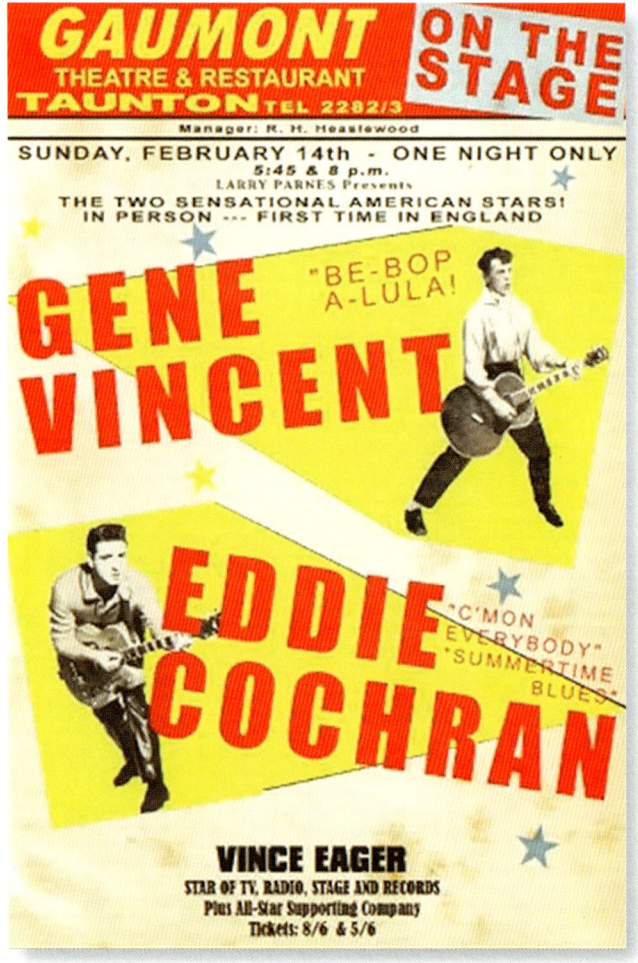

MEET THE GUE

EMILE FORD
Special Guest Attraction

EMILE was born in the West Indies 22 years ago, one of a family of five (he has three brothers and a sister). His stepfather became Chief Crown Land Surveyor in the Bahamas, and the family lived there for five years.

Two years later the family set sail for England, with Emile determined to become an engineer. He worked for nine months as a porter to pay for his education.

Discovering that he had a natural aptitude for guitar-playing, he started making appearances in a London coffee bar, where he also started to develop as a singer. He soon formed his own accompanying group, The Checkmates.

They were booked for one or two minor television programmes, and at a regular Thursday night session at London's Lyceum Ballroom. But it was the winning of a talent competition at the Soho Fair last summer which proved their lucky break, for it won them a Pye disc contract.

Emile and The Checkmates waxed "What Do You Want To Make Those Eyes At Me For," which became the nation's No. 1 favourite. Their second disc, "Slow Boat To China," has climbed to No. 5 position.

They recently starred in a regular ATV series, "Sunday Serenade," and are featured every Tuesday lunchtime in BBC Light Programme's "Pop Shop."

Page Fourteen

STARS

EDDIE COCHRAN
Special Guest Attraction

...born on October 3, 1938, in ...ma City. He moved to ...ilst still a youngster, and later ...ttled in California. He has ...and two sisters.

...f music goes back to early ...en, as the youngest member ..., his sisters used to put him ...renading him with "Roll Out ...n the gramophone. He suffered ...ent, when he was accidentally ...g during a hunting trip—but ...his months in hospital that ...become a singer.

...oduced to Jerry Capehart, who ...was associated with Liberty ...ollywood.

...ord, "Sittin' In The Balcony" ...ciable success in America, and ...eing signed for a part in the ...d film, "The Girl Can't Help ...e sang "Twenty Flight Rock." ...table entries in Britain include ...Blues," "C'mon Everybody," ...se" and currently "Hallelujah, ...o."

Congratulations
TO EMI ARTISTS
on your achievements in the
NEW MUSICAL EXPRESS POLL

THE JOHN BARRY SEVEN	THE KING BROTHERS
SHIRLEY BASSEY	THE MUDLARKS
CHRIS BARBER	RUBY MURRAY
EDDIE CALVERT	THE PLATTERS
ALMA COGAN	THE PONI-TAILS
RUSS CONWAY	CLIFF RICHARD
THE DALLAS BOYS	THE SHADOWS
ELLA FITZGERALD	FRANK SINATRA
CONNIE FRANCIS	MONTY SUNSHINE

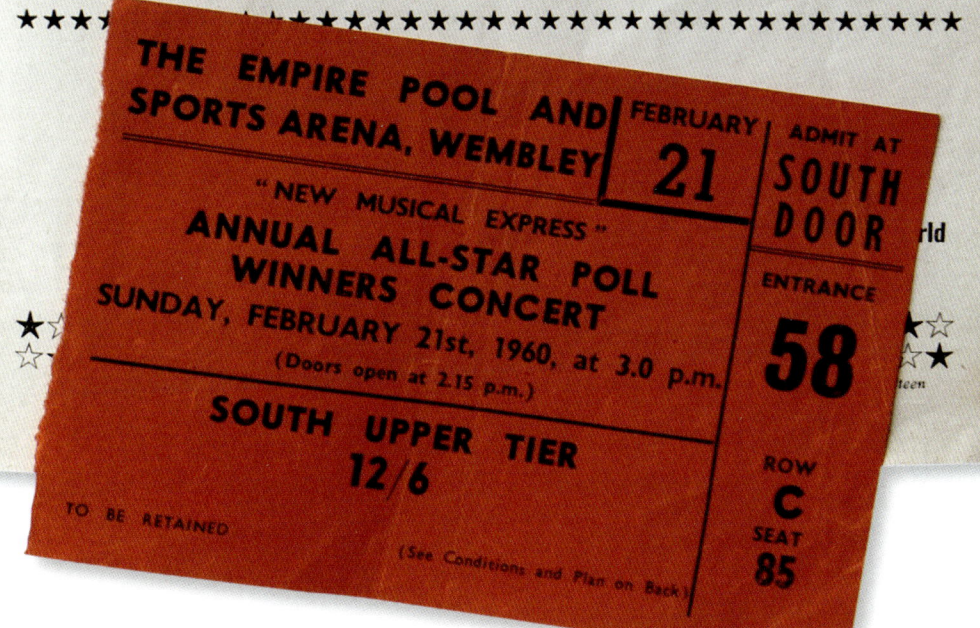

THE EMPIRE POOL AND SPORTS ARENA, WEMBLEY
FEBRUARY 21
ADMIT AT SOUTH DOOR

"NEW MUSICAL EXPRESS"
ANNUAL ALL-STAR POLL WINNERS CONCERT
SUNDAY, FEBRUARY 21st, 1960, at 3.0 p.m.
(Doors open at 2.15 p.m.)

SOUTH UPPER TIER
12/6

ENTRANCE 58
ROW C
SEAT 85

TO BE RETAINED
(See Conditions and Plan on Back)

(Opposite) Eddie during the recording of the ABC TV show *Boy Meets Girls* in Manchester on 15 January 1960, which was broadcast the following evening.

(Top) Selby's Restaurant in London's Hanover Street at an ABC TV press buffet on 13 January 1960. In attendance, along with Eddie and Billy Fury, were Jack Good, Craig Douglas, Joe Brown and Vernon Girl Lynn Cornett.

(Bottom) Eddie recording another appearance on *Boy Meets Girls*, this time on 19 February.

Rehearsing for *Boy Meets Girls* on 19 February 1960.

Eddie in his prime at the *NME* Poll Winners Party concert, Wembley Empire Pool on 21 February 1960.

Chapter Twenty-two

*I*T WAS COLD when they got to Coventry on 28 January. The tour was there for the first of four one-nighters in a row, starting at the Gaumont Theatre. The audience was great and the reception Eddie got warmed him up some but he was starting to think of home and he was starting to miss the sunshine. A few drinks after the show should help with that. The next night, at Worcester Gaumont, he was playing to a big house. There were 1,800 seats in the joint and Eddie and his band were clicking and the audience were screaming and hollering.

When the tour hit Bradford on 30 January, Gene decided to slow things down a little and give the crowd his version of 'Over The Rainbow'. The crowd didn't want it and let Gene know in no uncertain terms that they were not there to hear him croon. They yelled for Eddie to come back on and Gene walked off, cutting short his set and not reappearing until the final number with the rest of the cast. Vince Eager and Eddie came on to give the crowd what they wanted as Gene skulked backstage, they took the stage, stole the show and saved the night. Eddie started to drink more and call home more and the phone calls started getting expensive. He was dealing with time difference and culture shock and he was still processing grief, he was tired and he was wide awake. He called Shrimper again. He told her that the next night's gig was 250 miles away, in Southampton.

Britain was grey, it never got light during the day, not properly, not like he was used to, and Eddie was starting to feel like the tour was wearing him down a little. The next day his face was pressed up against a bus window. Around him the band and crew were laughing and smoking, they were talking about the girls they met last night and how wild the crowd was. Outside the window there was a canal, there were houseboats with smoke at their chimneys. Behind them a steep valley-side dotted with stone houses rose into a grey sky. He thought of Sharon again. He heard the sound of her laughter again.

Eddie was coughing on stage in Southampton and girls were being hauled away from the front of the stage by local cops. Maybe Eddie's cough was from cigarettes and booze and late nights or maybe he'd picked something up on the road, or maybe it was both. He was travelling to and from gigs with everyone, they were either on trains for the longer journeys or buses for the short hops. The distances they were covering were too long. When they left Southampton they headed to Glasgow, over 400 miles away. Eddie and Gene were travelling first class and the band were travelling third but soon they were all getting together and Eddie was playing his guitar and Joe Brown was playing his and people were singing along and adding rhythm on whatever was around and suddenly it was a party.

Eddie had been on the UK charts pretty much since he got there, his 'Hallelujah I Love Her So' was currently at number 22. The fact that the song had appeared in two consecutive episodes of *Boy Meets Girls* hadn't hurt. It was late. Eddie had been sitting up with Joe Brown, playing guitars and singing songs, but Joe left so he called Sharon again, then he called Shrimper again. It was a long run in Glasgow. The shows earlier in the week were quieter but they were still putting in two performances a day and Eddie still had his cough. The weekend shows were the money-spinners, the crowds were bigger and wilder, they'd got a day to recover and were determined to make the most of Gene and Eddie. Eddie didn't disappoint, he'd got his act down by the time he played in Glasgow. He opened with his back to the audience, rolling his shoulders as he built a riff on his 6120, the band behind him lit as silhouettes from behind a curtain. He built the riff and built the riff until he filled the room with it and the curtain lifted and he turned to face the crowd and 'Somethin' Else' kicked in for real and the crowd went wild and that was all she wrote. The next day, Gene Vincent was screaming at a hotel manager. He was screaming that he'd been robbed and that he was gonna sue this goddamn hotel for a million bucks. Gene hadn't been robbed and he wouldn't sue anyone, but he had been a pain in the ass all day so Eddie had gone and hidden his leg-iron and Gene was on fire about the whole thing.

Eddie was drunk again in the middle of the day, drunker than he realised. He was racking up another huge international phone bill just to connect with home. On the other end of the line was Sharon, she was wearing shades and she was in California and she was talking about how hot it was there, unable to comprehend how Eddie was feeling, how his long afternoons were filled with nothing to do but drink and miss home and play his records. The rain kept pouring. Even if there was somewhere to go it was too cold and too grey, it got dark by mid-afternoon and the hours were starting to stretch. There was always the booze though, to help chew up the hours. Eddie thought about Jerry, about what was going to happen there. It was the longest time he'd been away from him since they met, their partnership was dissolving and there was talk of legal proceedings. Then Eddie was in first class with Gene again. The train was pulling into Sheffield station and they were getting their things together. They met fans at the gig, competition winners, then a small group of local kids gawped at the eagle on the back of Eddie's leather and he let one of them try it on. Tickets for the good *Fast Moving Beat Show* seats, the ones down front, cost eight shillings and sixpence. Joe Cocker, a local with a voice, had saved for weeks for his. Eddie closed the first half of the show and gave Joe and the rest of the crowd exactly what they wanted. They got the full punk rock rumble of 'Somethin' Else' and the silver waistcoat, they got 'What'd I Say' and they got 'Twenty Flight Rock'. The audience were up and out of their seats, they were ecstatic, wild. Every move Eddie made was the right move, every note he played was the right note and the band behind him were in lock step, anticipating him when he needed them to and following his lead from first riff to last. Eddie slicked his hair back between songs and coughed now and then.

The day before Valentine's, Eddie and Gene were back in the rented flat in Jermyn Street. They'd got a few days off then a gig pretty close to where they were staying. The next theatre they played, at the Granada in Woolwich, was the craziest venue yet, there was a hall of mirrors and a grand staircase and an eager crowd forming outside. Eddie's throat was still sore and he was still coughing despite the whiskey and honey he was drinking for medicinal purposes, but the show had to go on so Eddie's changed it up and ran onto the stage rather than starting with his back to the crowd. Later, Eddie was calling home again. He was telling Shrimper that 'the gigs in the UK are great but some of the days are so long, mama.' He didn't tell Shrimper about the nights, when the shows were finished and the after party was finished and he was in another lonely room thinking about Ritchie and Buddy or he was having to step in and break up the fight between Gene and whoever Gene was mad at. He didn't tell Shrimper that he'd been drinking way more, maybe too much, that it was helping him to get to sleep and it was helping him to stay awake.

After their Valentine's Day show at the Gaumont Theatre in Taunton, Eddie and Gene recorded for *Brian Matthews Parade of Pops* radio show together for the BBC and Eddie was amused by their single mic and lo-fi recording setup. Once they finished up the session they met Billy Fury and headed back up to Manchester with Billy and road manager Hal Carter to record more *Boy Meets Girls* episodes. Eddie and Gene were drinking all the way to Manchester, slugging Scotch from the bottle with a Coca-Cola chaser. Eddie was drunk and mischievous and when they got to the hotel he decided he needed comic books, he needed Hal to go out and find him a bunch of comic books. Hal tried, but it was late afternoon and it was 1960 in Manchester and the best he could come up with were a few magazines. The next morning, they were taping their performances for a couple more episodes of Jack Good's show with Billy Fury, Adam Faith and Jess Conrad. When they got to the studio, Jack Good had gone to town. The set and the lighting were class, and Eddie, head to toe in leather, responded by looking and sounding like he belonged there.

Eddie Cochran and Gene Vincent were fire and ice, two very different characters with some insight into each other's worlds, bonded by circumstance and genuine camaraderie. Their next stop was Leicester on 18 February, where *The Fast Moving Beat Show* was booked to play the De Montfort Hall. Vince Eager was on the bill and he brought his mother along and she brought her homemade apple tart along that Eddie had been craving since he first tried it weeks back. Once the tart had been eaten and the gig had been played, Gene and Eddie had to head straight back to Manchester to finish up the filming for Jack Good where they taped a duet together, a version of the Big Bopper's 'White Lightning'. Taping done, Eddie and Gene headed off together again, to play Dundee the next night. The gig went so well that the police were called in to control the uncontrollable crowd. Fights broke out and people rushed the stage while Gene was up there. Eddie, Gene and Vince Eager made their getaway from the chaos by being snuck out of the basement to a waiting car, then Eddie and Gene hightailed it the five hundred plus miles from Dundee back to London for the *New Musical Express* Poll Winners gig in Wembley where Eddie pulled out his checked shirt, metallic waistcoat and leather pants and blew the crowd away.

The morning after the *NME* performance, Eddie started two days of recording for the BBC again, this time at Maida Vale, for their *Parade Of The Pops* show where Eddie ran through 'C'Mon Everybody' and 'Milk Cow Blues'. The day after the recordings were in the can, Eddie was off again, to join the *Beat Show* at The Globe in Stockton-On-Tees for a one-nighter. Eddie was bored of the train grind now, he'd had enough of travelling from cold, wet, grey platform to cold, wet, grey platform and the towns were all starting to look the same. He played up on the train, he pulled the emergency cord for kicks and paid the five pounds fine on the spot. He then upgraded Vince and a few of the other guys to First Class so they could join him there and pass a bottle around and sing and play and make the trip more fun.

It was cold and Eddie was a long way from home, but his act was getting better every night. It was what his day was built around. All the tedious hours of travel on trains and buses, all the nondescript hotels and bed and breakfast joints, they were all so Eddie could do his thing twice a night, so he could cut loose on the guitar breaks in his scarlet shirt, waistcoat and leather pants and hear the crowd whoop and holler. The UK fans were great. Eddie made time for them after the gigs, he hung out, talked with them, signed autographs and posed for photos. After a much needed day off he was on his way to Wales, to meet the Beat Show on 26 February at the Cardiff Gaumont. In Cardiff they'd waited too long for Gene and Eddie and raised the roof when they hit the stage. It was an electrifying night, another electrifying night. Then it was over and the after party was over and Eddie was alone again, coming down and missing home, seeing the story in the papers about the plane that just crashed in Ireland and thinking about Buddy, Ritchie and JP. The Cardiff show was the last one-nighter, it was week-long residencies in seven different cities from there on out.

1960 was a leap year and on 29 February Eddie was on the train to Leeds with the guys. They were excited about the shows, Joe Brown was on the bill, so was Billy Fury. Joe had been with Larry Parnes for a while and he was using his spot on the tour to promote his latest single, 'Darktown Strutters' Ball'. Larry Parnes and Jack Good had spotted Joe when he was playing guitar on 'Oh Boy!' They noted his natural ability and his easy way with an audience and thought they could turn it into something, so they did. Joe was a little different than most of Larry's acts, Joe stood up for himself and never took the first offer as he hammered out his deals with Larry. Joe looked the part too, he'd got himself a Gibson 335 and spiky blond hair and a leather jacket with fur at the collar

Advertising for the upcoming week of shows running from 14 to 19 March 1960 at the Liverpool Empire.

like Eddie's. Billy Fury was one of Parnes's most successful acts. Larry had discovered him up in New Brighton, at a Marty Wilde show. Billy was raw back then but his talent was unquestionable. He wore a gold suit like Elvis and he was starting to hit the charts every time he put out a record. His latest tune was another that he'd written himself, called 'Collette', and it was currently climbing the UK chart where it would peak at number nine.

Tour manager Hal Carter made his way to Eddie and Gene's hotel to pick them up for the first show of the day in Leeds at the Empire where they were performing between 29 February and 5 March, but Eddie and Gene had been drinking together. Eddie had been keeping up with Gene, matching him drink for drink, and by the time Hal arrived he was wasted, so wasted that he needed to try to sleep it off for a while when he got to the venue. He didn't sleep it off, not really, but he played the gig for the fans who were still showing up in droves despite some of the snotty reviews the tour was getting. The gig went well, although when he finally sobered up, Eddie had no memory of it whatsoever. Eddie's boozing wasn't going unnoticed, even in the heady atmosphere of a travelling rock'n'roll tour. According to Vince Eager:

…when he drank, he drank to excess… he drank more when he did the weekly shows than he did when he did the one-nighters. When you're doing weeks you're in digs, you get bored, you've got all day to hang around and he was spending fortunes on the phone and drinking a lot.

Back at the digs in Leeds, Gene turned up in his underwear. His cab from the gig had been surrounded by fans who'd torn at him and torn at him until they'd got the souvenir they were looking for, his leather pants.

The cold and damp were still clinging to Eddie's clothes, still turning to steam at the venues or in front of the three bar fire back in his room. The hours alone were dragging man, they were stretching out and leaving him feeling lonely. He took another drink, made another phone call home. He got back to his room just as British TV shut down for the night and lay on his bed and the dark thoughts came so he tried to drink them away but that only made them worse. He schlepped through the never-ending British winter from Gaumonts to Empires, another town and another room. Another lace curtain and another bad meal.

Gene and Eddie travelled first class to Birmingham to play the Hippodrome, where they were booked from 7 to 12 March, which was where they started to rotate the bill. Eddie found himself now closing the whole show, in Gene's old headliner spot, and he was worried how Gene was going to take it. Gene was still setting crowds on fire but Eddie was the guy with the recent hits. Eddie wasn't as malevolent as Gene, he was easier to like. Eddie took to the stage in Birmingham with his shades on. His eyes were straining, they were tired and ringed from the late nights and the booze and he'd still got the remnants of the black eye that Gene gave him when one of their fights got a little out of hand. The on-the-road hijinks to pass the time and kill the boredom were ramping up. Hal arrived at a hotel one night to find the manager screaming at him. He was screaming because pretty much all of his chambermaids were partying with Eddie and Gene the night before and a bunch of them were still secreted away, hiding in their double room somewhere. The red-faced hotel manager had had enough, his was a respectable establishment and the two American rock'n'roll stars were going to have to return his staff to him and find alternative accommodation immediately. They found it, or rather Hal found it, in the shape of a homely little local bed and breakfast that didn't come with partying chambermaids, and they spent the rest of their stay in the city there. Gene was getting more unpredictable, he'd named his switchblade Henry and he started pulling it out and waving it around when he'd spent a night on the liquor, which was pretty much every night. On one occasion he took the blade to Hal Carter's suit and put some slices in it while Hal was still wearing it.

Eddie and Gene packed up their things and checked out of the bed and breakfast and headed to Liverpool for a week of shows at the Empire from 14 to 18 March. The travel days were the fun days. It was crazy really, the whole load of them travelling by train but there was something bonding about those days. They broke the monotony. They cut through the rain and the bad food and there were good times to be had if you knew where to look. And Eddie still knew where to look. Gypsy Rosalee was heading to Liverpool too. She was going there from Blackpool where she gave psychic consultations by the sea to read Eddie's future backstage. Eddie's readings were given and pictures were taken to hang on her Blackpool wall and if she saw any problems in Eddie's immediate

Gene Vincent Joe Brown Billy Fury Eddie Cochran

(Left) Gene, Joe, Billy and Eddie in the dressing room at the Manchester Hippodrome.

(Right) At the Green Room Restaurant above the Sheffield Gaumont Theatre on 7 February 1960, with members of the Sheffield Star's Teenage Club.

future, then Gypsy Rosalee didn't warn him about them. After one Liverpool show, Eddie and Gene were doing an interview for local radio. Eddie sounded rough and the crowd were still screaming in the background and Eddie was still plugging 'Hallelujah I Love Her So', even though it no longer had a home on the charts. The Liverpool shows were a knock-out. Out in the audience, a young George Harrison watched in awe at the nonchalance and deep cool with which Eddie greeted a girl in the crowd.

The *Fast Moving Beat Show* was highs 'n' lows, it was fasts 'n' slows, it was screams and then it was silence, and it was really starting to get to Eddie. The international phone calls home weren't cheap, he was racking up huge bills everywhere he stayed. The phone became his escape from the relentless grey of the long days waiting to play a show. The next stop on the tour was Newcastle Empire from 21 to 26 March, Eddie was still wearing his shades and they became part of the act which despite it all, was still getting better every night. But Eddie was missing the feel of the sun on his face and Shrimper's cornbread and beans. He was missing the familiarity of home. The gigs were fabulous, the British audiences were wild, they got it, and for that brief, shining period every night, Eddie's demons were quelled and it all made sense. But the days were so long. Now the tour was solely booked for week long engagements they were longer still without the hustle of the travel between venues to fill them. Eddie's favoured non-musical pursuits, going hunting with his friends and a couple of cases of beer or hanging out with Sharon or his family weren't open to him. In the austere, bed and breakfast Britain of 1960, Eddie's girlfriend, his family and his Californian home felt a long way away.

Gene got a new cast on his leg. What was once cold metal was now plaster but the change did nothing to ease Gene's mood. It was 2 a.m. again somewhere and the stage make-up had worn off. Eddie was on the telephone to Sharon again. She was still in California, still wearing sunglasses as convertibles drove past her window. Eddie's words were slurring, he'd been drinking too much again. He'd been hanging out with Gene and drinking and jumping in to calm things down when Gene threatened someone or someone threatened Gene. Sharon asked him where he was and he said he wasn't sure, Ipswich maybe, or Newcastle. No, not Ipswich. The opening night of the tour was in Ipswich. Newcastle. He was pretty sure he was in Newcastle. It wasn't Newcastle for long though. Pretty soon the whole show hit the road again and headed to Manchester for their residency at the Hippodrome that would take them from 28 March to 2 April. When Sharon finally flew in to meet Eddie in Manchester, the trip was business and pleasure. Canny as ever, while she was in the UK Sharon was booked in to record a tune called 'Homework' over at Decca Records. Eddie seemed different from the last time Sharon had seen him. He wore his leathers and his make-up when they posed for snaps backstage in Manchester with Billy Fury and Sharon could see plain as day that the weeks on the road were taking their toll on him. Gene was feeling it too. When he collapsed at the end of one of the Manchester shows, the doctor who attended him diagnosed the rocker with pleurisy. He ignored Gene's protestations that he was fine to carry on, and prescribed bed rest. Three days later Gene Vincent was risen and dragging his busted leg across the Manchester Hippodrome stage. Part of Gene's showman schtick involved Joe Brown bending down so Gene could swing his leg over his head. One time, Joe didn't crouch low enough or Gene didn't swing high enough and Joe took one to the side of the head and ended up flat out on the stage with his Gibson beneath him. No matter how the musicians were feeling though, no matter how much they brooded and drank, the shows just kept getting better and the crowds kept getting wilder.

Chapter Twenty-three

EDDIE HAD SHARON go out and buy a bunch of Buddy Holly records and started playing them on repeat, feeding his dark premonitions and working through his grief. It was the first time Eddie had been able to listen to Buddy since the crash and now he was listening to him over and over, sitting in front of the record player while Sharon looked on, concerned for Eddie but unable to break through the wall of grief he was building between himself and the world. There's a story from the tour which may or may not be true, that came originally from hotel manager Arnold Burlin. One night in Manchester when Sharon was asleep, Eddie was awake and downstairs, crazy with booze and grief and banging on the hotel manager's door. When the first confused and then terrified manager opened the door, Eddie grabbed hold of him and screamed at him that he was going to die and that there was nothing anyone could do to stop it. Eddie was inconsolable and didn't calm down until a doctor was called to shoot him up with a sedative. Whatever private hell Eddie was going through on the tour, he was still hiding it from the fans and fulfilling his role as showman and star twice a night, every night. He made a personal appearance at a Manchester record store for ravenous fans and laughed as he watched cops try to hold them back. Eddie and Gene got invited over to Oldham, just outside of Manchester, to add some American star power to a local beauty contest where they happily posed for pictures with an array of British beauty queens. The photos of Eddie and Gene at the beauty pageant show the effect the tour was having on Eddie, he looks wasted in the pictures, like he's not fully there. He's tired, his eyes are bloodshot and his face is starting to bloat a little. Once the Manchester dates were done and the town's thirst for rock'n'roll was sated, Eddie headed back with Sharon, Gene and the gang to London, where they were playing a residency in Finsbury Park. The Everly Brothers had just arrived in the UK to start their own tour and Duane Eddy was in town too. Once the London gigs were done on 9 April, Eddie, Sharon, Gene and the whole *Fast Moving Beat Show* gang headed down to Bristol to finish up the first leg of the tour dates. Eddie was excited, once the Bristol dates were done he got to fly home, he got to see Alice and the family and feel the warm California sun on his face. Sharon was excited too, a trip home would do Eddie good, it'd help him with whatever this was that he was going through. Eddie still seemed different to Sharon, altered. He'd been hanging out with Gene far too much and drinking far too much and doing whatever else he did on the road far too much. Sharon was a realist, she knew the reality of rock'n'roll, its temptations and frustrations, every bit as well as Eddie, it was her world as much as it was his, and she thought that Eddie needed a break.

The Bristol shows started out weird. Marty Wilde had been booked at the last minute for a prestigious TV show and Larry Parnes pulled his band off the shows so they could back Marty on the TV. Larry hadn't been to a single show on the whole tour, he'd received daily updates and solved any problems that came up by phone but never showed up in person. There was a gap in the Bristol schedule for Good Friday and then suddenly, after week upon gruelling week on the road, there was only one more gig to do. The plane tickets to the US got delivered to Gene and Eddie's room and Eddie was on the phone to Shrimper again. He was telling her to stock up on cornbread and beans, he was telling her that the first leg of the tour was almost done and that her boy would be home soon, sleeping in his own bed. Eddie wowed the Bristol crowd. He started his show with his back to them, shaking his leather hips and rolling his shoulders as he played the riff to 'Somethin' Else' with Sharon watching from the side of the stage as the rockers rocked, the Teddy Boys bopped and the jivers jived.

Eddie had been hitting the stage and plugging in the 6120 for months. Nights off were few and far between and as much as parts of the tour had been a blast, California was calling and all Eddie wanted to do was head for home. As soon as the last *Beat Show* gig was done, Eddie could leave, he could head to London and board a plane with Sharon to take them back to California, back to Shrimper, back to Buena Park. He started to plan how to get to London, Johnny Gentle was heading that way but his car was full already, so someone suggested that they use Ace Taxis, the firm that had been running people around all week. They booked the cab to get them to the airport and had it wait for them at the venue, Ace Taxis sent their guy and the luggage was loaded into the trunk. Eddie avoided the fans waiting for a glimpse of him by slipping out of the side door and before long he, Sharon and Gene were climbing into the back of the taxi as show manager Patrick Thompkins got in up front on the bench-seat, next to the driver. Sharon and Eddie were on a high, singing 'California Here We Come' as the car started out for London, its back seat still dotted with confetti from the newlyweds it had carried earlier in the day. Gene had taken a bunch of downers and was out cold. Eddie had his arm around Sharon's shoulder, he pulled her toward him and she pulled him toward her. They were tired but they were exhilarated. Eddie hated to fly but at least Sharon was there with him to take his mind off the flight. Don't think about J.P., Eddie. Don't think about Ritchie or Buddy, don't think about Clear Lake.

The Ace Taxi cab driver's name was George Martin, he was 19 years old and had been backstage drinking beer with Eddie and Gene at least one of the Bristol shows. The car he was driving was a Ford Consul Mark Two Deluxe in cream n' chrome, and he was driving it too fast. George was amped up, he had rock'n'roll stars in the back of his car with somewhere important to be and he was going to get them there fast. Sharon started asking if the tyres on the Consul could handle the kinds of speeds he was doing, he was taking corners too quick and tight and not slowing down and the 'California Here We Come' singing had stopped. Patrick reached for his cigarettes up front and Sharon got increasingly worried in back. Then George took a wrong turn and got flustered, wanting to do this job, of all jobs, right. He floored the Ford to make up time and headed into a corner doing 50mph.

The Ford Consul Deluxe clipped the kerb and all hell broke loose in slow motion. One of the car's tyres got busted and went flat fast. Meanwhile the car, now skidding on the newly laid gravel road surface, was getting thrown to the other side of the street. Then it was spinning and skidding and it was out of George's control. Gene was still asleep and they were about to hit a lamppost. Eddie was sitting between Sharon and Gene and he saw the lamppost coming straight at Sharon, so he leaned across her to try to protect her, but then the door opened and they were thrown from the car. There were cries in the air and the sound of crunching metal and then for a moment it was silent apart from Sharon's low moans.

As the street lights illuminating the crash were extinguished for the night and the scene went dark, George and Patrick were shook up but they were OK. Gene, Eddie and Sharon were all in a bad way, laying contorted and broken on a patch of grass, metres away from the car. Gene and Sharon were conscious, Sharon was still moaning in pain and Gene was quiet. Eddie was quiet too. Eddie was just lying there. Cars started stopping and people started to gather. Police and ambulances were called and George and Patrick were still dazed. Two policemen arrived at midnight followed by an ambulance fifteen minutes later. It was one in the morning when the ambulance got Eddie, Sharon and Gene to the hospital where Doctor Pilton oversaw their care. Gene had busted his collarbone and his leg, the source of so much of his pain, was way worse now. Sharon's pelvis was broken and they started looking to ascertain the extent of her head and back injuries. But Eddie, Eddie was still just lying there. He was unresponsive and the doctors started using words like 'brain trauma' and 'severe'. Gene and Sharon had responded to treatment and the staff were hopeful that the two of them would recover. Eddie was still unconscious and unresponsive. The signs were all bad and then they got worse. Then, at ten minutes past four on the afternoon of Easter Sunday, 17 April 1960, Eddie Cochran, the kid from Albert Lea, silently slipped away from us with his eyes closed, and was pronounced dead.

Cyril Pugh, the proprietor of Pugh's Garage on Bath Road, Chippenham where the wrecked Ford Consul Mark II was towed after the crash.

...day, April 22, 1960

The cruel tragedy of ED[DIE]

TRIBUTES have poured in—from fellow artists, business colleagues, friends and countless thousands of saddened fans. All have been shocked into deep mourning by the sudden, tragic death of American rock 'n' roll star Eddie Cochran in a road accident early on Sunday morning, just before he was due to return to America to get married.

Most heartfelt tribute of all came from the lips of singer Gene Vincent, who was also injured in the same crash. Completely heartbroken at the loss of his best friend, Gene told me quietly and sincerely: "He was the greatest guy I ever knew. I'm going to miss him so very much."

The accident occurred at Chippenham, Wiltshire, when the chauffeur-driven car in which Eddie, Gene, Hollywood songwriter Sharon Sheeley and tour manager Pat Thompkins were travelling to London Airport skidded into a lamp standard after a tyre burst.

All four were thrown out into the road. They were rushed to St. Martin's Hospital, Bath, but Eddie never recovered consciousness and was too weak to undergo a brain operation, despite the efforts of doctors who battled to save his life.

Vincent, who sustained multiple head injuries and a fractured collar bone, was not told of Eddie's death until Monday.

Injured GENE VINCENT pays tribute to pal

as he talks to KEITH GOODWIN

Fiancee

In another ward of the Bath hospital, Sharon Sheeley—writer of Ricky Nelson's first major British hit, "Poor Little Fool"—is being treated for severe back injuries and a suspected broken pelvis.

Sharon (20) came here only a few weeks ago to join Eddie on his one-night-stand tour.

On Tuesday night she had recovered sufficiently to make this statement: "Eddie and I were officially and secretly engaged two years ago. We told no one because Eddie didn't want his teen-age fans to know. We were to be married in Hollywood on Saturday."

Eddie and Gene were returning to America for a short "working holiday" prior to more British dates beginning next month. Only two weeks ago, Eddie told me: "I'm so homesick that I feel I just have to get back to the States for a few days..."

The body of 21-year-old Oklahoma-born Eddie was due to be flown on Thursday to his California home for the funeral service at the Artists' Cemetery in Hollywood. He is survived by his mother and father, a brother and three sisters.

A brilliant guitarist, Eddie began singing by accident a few years ago when he auditioned for a minor role in the "big beat" film "The Girl Can't Help It." After signing with the U.S. Liberty label, he won Gold Discs for million-plus sales of "Twenty Flight Rock" and "Sittin' In The Balcony."

Eddie notched his first British hit in 1958 with "Summertime Blues," his own composition. In addition to arranging the tune, he also sang the solo vocal, handled the bass voice heard now and then, and by multi-recording techniques, played piano, bass, guitar and drums on the disc.

He played three instruments on his second hit here—guitar, bass and drums. The tune was another of his originals titled "C'mon Everybody," and it enjoyed a long run in the best sellers.

On his most recent hit—"Hallelujah I Love Her So," which was featured in the charts earlier this year—he played piano. Many critics hailed this as his greatest recording.

Due for release on May 6 is Eddie's next record—a disc with the ironic title "Three Steps To Heaven." Although the reverse coupling has not yet been announced, it is possible that the record will now be issued earlier.

Eddie made his British debut on ABC-TV's "Boy Meets Girls" in January, and later joined Gene Vincent for a lengthy one-night-stand concert tour, interspersed with variety dates. Along with Vincent, he was a special guest star at the annual NME Poll-Winners Concert in February.

Eddie's projected 10 days in America this month were to have been taken up with concerts, TV dates and discussions for a major Hollywood film set for production later this year. In addition to "The Girl Can't Help It," he has previously appeared in such films as "Untamed Youth" and the forthcoming "Johnny Melody."

Unbelievable

Still sorely grief-stricken, Gene Vincent (25) talked to me about his "buddy" on Tuesday. "I still can't believe it's true. You see, it seems so strange now. Eddie and I were rarely apart. I keep wanting to call out for him.

"They told me that I kept asking for him in the hospital, but I didn't find out exactly what happened until last night. What can I say?

"I'm still trying to get over it. But I don't think I ever will," he said quietly.

Gene told me he was leaving for America at noon on Wednesday so that he can attend the funeral. "I feel I have to be there," he emphasised.

What about his British dates? "I'll go through with them. There won't be any cancellations," he assured me.

GENE VINCENT'S tribute to EDDIE COCHRAN

EDDIE ... always cheer[ful]

INQUEST

AT THE INQUEST AT ... was informed that bra... killed Eddie Cochran, w... inquest was adjourned ... was flown home on We... his home in Hollywo... VINCENT and SHAR... Cochran in the same car ... "progressing slowly"...

And here he is with the DEC... right: BOB CRAB...

...E COCHRAN

One of Eddie's closest friends ...Britain was singer **Vince Eager**, ...o was to have met the stars at ...ondon Airport to journey with ...em to America as Eddie's guest. ...was thought at one time that ...nce would accompany Eddie's ...dy to the States, but Vince has ...ce declined.

"It wouldn't be right, because ...really don't think I could give ...uch comfort to his parents at a ...ne like this," he explained, ...sely.

"Eddie was a wonderful ...ellow," Vince went on. "He liked everybody and consequently they loved him. He always got on so well with fans. I've never known him to refuse an autograph or complain about being in a hurry when a fan stopped him. He really liked meeting people.

"Of course," continued Vince, ...he was a great artist—a real ...rd worker. He had faith in me ...an artist and helped me in ...ery possible way with my act. ...m telling you, Eddie was the ...atest. I'll miss him—believe ...e, I will," he added fervently.

Another young British star who ...orked with Eddie on stage and ...V is **Billy Fury**, who told me: ...Eddie was one of the most ...namic performers I've ever seen ...stage. I was pretty close to ...m and this has upset me more ...an I can tell you. I'll always ...member him as a very talented ...d very wonderful fellow."

Singer-guitarist **Joe Brown**, who ...orked alongside Eddie on the ...Boy Meets Girls" shows, told ...e: "He was one of the greatest of all the rock 'n' rollers. And he was certainly the greatest guitarist I've ever heard. As a person, he was a wonderful fellow—simply wonderful."

Eddie played his final British engagement last week at Bristol Hippodrome, where one of the British artists on the bill was **Johnny Gentle**. Recapping on the time he spent with the American singer, Johnny said: "He struck me as being a person who really enjoyed life, and it was always a pleasure to be with him."

Ironic

The final ironic twist is that Eddie, Gene, Sharon and Pat Thompkins originally planned to travel to London by train, and only decided to hire a car at the last minute.

"Eddie told me he had booked a car because he thought it would be quicker than train," Johnny Gentle said.

"Peter Wynn and myself left by car before him," he went on, "but just outside Chippenham, we found we were running short of petrol and turned back to find a garage. Later we saw the wreckage of a car, but didn't think to enquire about the passengers," he added.

And so the pop music world has lost another very talented young star. But thousands of fans all over the world, who now join us in offering our deepest sympathy to his family and friends, will make sure that Eddie Cochran isn't forgotten.

TRAGEDY

A RECORD & SHOW MIRROR picture of EDDIE COCHRAN taken the day he arrived in London the first week in January this year.

TRAGEDY STRUCK the world of rock 'n' roll on Easter Sunday, when American performer Eddie Cochran—who had just ended a tour of Britain —died in St. Martin's Hospital, Bath, where he had been taken a few hours earlier after being in a car crash.

It was the most shattering news to reach fans of beat music since the deaths in a plane crash last year of Buddy Holly, Big Bopper and Ritchie Valens.

Cochran had completed his British tour at Bristol on Easter Saturday night, and was in a chauffeur-driven hire car headed for London Airport.

There he was due to take a plane back to America, to help in the promotion of his new disc release, "Three Steps To Heaven."

Also in the car were Sharon Sheeley, a songwriter, who was a close friend of Cochran's; Gene Vincent, another American beat singer, who had been appearing with him and agent Patrick Thompkins. They suffered comparatively minor injuries, and—at the time of going to press— were reported as "comfortable."

Vince Eager, British rock performer, had been waiting at the airport to fly to America with Cochran—as his guest. When he heard the news, he cancelled his flight, and was planning to travel in the plane that took Cochran's body back to America for burial.

...DJOURNED

...n Tuesday, the coroner ...s in the car crash had ...ly 21 years of age. The ...ay 23. Cochran's body ...rom London Airport to ...st news about GENE ...ELEY, who were with ...crashed, is that they are ...ving their injuries.

...ls who gave him such a rousing welcome . . . left to ...SSELL-THOMPSON and PAT CAMPBELL.

TV STAR annual

Allen Case	84
Dick Clark	51
Eddie Cochran	7
Perry Como	89
Chuck Connors	87
Bob Conrad	12
Tim Considine	36
Jackie Cooper	60
Bing Crosby	89

GARDNE
EDDIE C
LUANA
TONY CU

THE FINAL CURTAIN

Three Steps to Heaven was, ironically, the last record ever made by 22-year-old Eddie Cochran. A blowout sent his London taxi crashing into a lamp post; he died on the operating table 16 hours later. For Hope Emerson ("Mother" on the Peter Gunn show, "Sarge" with Dennis O'Keefe) death came after months of illness with a liver ailment. The 6'2", 190-pound actress from Hawarden, Iowa was also noted as a "hot" piano player.

IN MEMORY OF EDDIE

"3 STEP TO HEAVEN

■ At the height of his career, 21-ye Cochran cut a record called "Three S Heaven." A week later, he was dea death was the result of a freak auto by a blowout, while he was en route Airport to return home after a sen week tour of Great Britain. Also i in the crash was his friend from c songwriter Sharon Sheeley. A star the age of 17, when his first hit, "Si the Balcony," was released by Liber one of the most popular of the youn roll performers. Shy and quiet, Eddi friends, but was admired by many. be deeply felt not only by his friends fans, but by the whole music indust

HAINES' HASSLE HITS
TOP TWENTY-FIVE

KVEN
1450 on your radio dial

Frank Haines
7 TIL 10 P.M.

VENTURA and SANTA BARBARA COUNTY'S FIRST RECORD SURVEY
Compiled from record sales, juke box plays and requests.

Week starting: **MONDAY, MAY 9, 1960**

NEW MOV LIF year

ALBUMS OF THE W
SANDS AT THE SANDS
LAUGHING ROOM
COOKE'S TOUR
EDDIE COCHRAN
DELLA BY STARLIGHT

OVIE LIFE

- Y: En Garde! 8
- "Three Steps To Heaven" 14
- JOHN SMITH: Congratulations! 18
- NET LEIGH: "Ain't It Wild" 20

A TEAR FOR GOOD-BYE: ZIMBALIST, McCLURE, LUCY-DESI, OLIVIER-LEIGH, LANZA, COCHRAN, BELVIN

DEATHS
- Joseph Cotten's wife Lenore Kipp .... Jan. 7
- Diana Barrymore .... Jan. 25
- Jesse Belvin .... Feb. 6
- Betty Lanza .... Mar. 11
- Ian Keith .... Mar. 26
- Eddie Cochran .... April 17
- Peter Breck's brother George .... May 29
- Edward Brophy .... May 30

Three Steps to Heaven was, ironically, the last record made by r. 'n' r. star Eddie Cochran before his death April 17 in an English auto crash. After a sensational tour, Eddie was enroute home with fiancée, songwriter Shari Sheeley, still hospitalized

Eddie at Decca House in London on 11 January 1960 during a reception held to introduce him to the UK press the day after he arrived in London. Renowned photographer Harry Hammond sent this portrait of Eddie to the Cochrans after Eddie's death.

Afterwards

I tell you, when I die I'm going to have a jam session…
The music will be played loud and it will be our music. I won't have any Beatles songs
but I'll have a few of Eddie Cochran's things and a whole lot of blues.
Jimi Hendrix, 1968

FOLLOWING THE CRASH, Eddie's body was flown back to the US and his funeral held at Forest Memorial Park in Cypress, California. Johnny Rook showed up at the new Cochran House in Buena Park and found a family destroyed. He was there when brother Bob and Red got back from meeting the casket at the airport and told Shrimper that the body laying there didn't even look like Eddie. Johnny stayed in Eddie's room while he was in Buena Park, surrounded by the remnants of his friend's life, so shattered by the tragedy that it would be decades before he could put a record on by his friend and listen to him play and sing again. Johnny was so cut up that he couldn't even face Eddie's funeral, he couldn't handle the sadness, trauma and grief and stayed instead in the silent Cochran house as Eddie was buried. Shrimper was, of course, devastated. She collapsed onto Eddie's casket at the funeral and wailed for her lost boy.

Alice wasn't alone in her heartbreak. As Monday dawned and word spread of Eddie's death, the world of rock'n'roll was once again left in shock and disbelief at the cruel twist of fate which had snatched away one of their very own, one of their rebel-rousers and pioneers. Newspapers carried pictures of the car wreck, the twisted metal and broken glass a stark indication of the senseless brutality of the crash. The news of Eddie's death was treated much as the plane crash in Clear Lake had been. Disbelief was followed by horror, then sadness and unending grief. Sharon Sheeley spent months recovering from the injuries she sustained on the way to London that night, replaying the incident over and over as she lay there. The car, the speed, the lamppost. She talked about Eddie, in his last conscious moments reaching out to save her, she said that the medic in the ambulance placed their hands together as they lay stretchered side by side en route to the hospital. There was little doubt in Sharon's mind that Eddie had saved her life and lost his own in the process. Sharon's friends rallied around her. Phil Everly, on tour in the UK with his brother, came by the hospital to visit, there were flowers in her room from Jack Good and Ricky Nelson and a collection of cuddly toys courtesy of Billy Fury. Eddie's fans wrote to Sharon too, they wrote to connect with her, to sympathise and empathise, to share their pain at losing Eddie, and Sharon understood. One fan sent a lovingly made scrapbook of Eddie's press cuttings and pictures. On one page were images from *The Girl Can't Help It*, Eddie and the Magnatone Maestro, looking so young and so alive on his first movie set. On another page was a portrait, Eddie staring straight into the camera, his hair piled high and tight, a half-smile on his lips. There were pictures of Eddie in his tweed sports coat and collar and tie and pictures of him in his leather pants.

Eddie Cochran was one of the reasons that rock'n'roll went on to change the whole wide world for a while. His songs tapped into universal themes, he gave a vocabulary to the mixed up feelings of teenagehood, he was beautiful and cool. Eddie lived in the crucible of a new dream. It was a cultural revolution happening in real time, no-one knew where it was headed or how long it would last, all anybody cared about was that it was here right now. It rode in on the back of new technologies like record players for the home and jukeboxes at the soda fountain and in-car radio and its sound spread like wildfire. Electric guitars, from affordable to expensive, were available from catalogues and music shops, topping thousands of kids' Christmas lists and fuelling their dreams. What people sometimes forgot amongst all the myth and romance, was that rock'n'roll was also a business. Larry Parnes had business at the top of his list of priorities when he decided that, despite Eddie's death, the show would go on.

The second leg of Parnes's *Fast Moving Beat Show* would continue, he decided, but be rebranded as an Eddie Cochran tribute show. Eddie's single, 'Three Steps To Heaven', was rush released and made an immediate b-line for the top of the charts so Parnes reasoned that the tour would pull in as many fans without Eddie as it had when he was headlining. It was too cynical a move for Vince Eager who had bonded so tightly with Eddie on the road. Vince had been waiting for Eddie at the airport after the crash, the morning that Eddie never showed up. Still numb with shock and grief, he quit the tour. Sharon, still unsteady on her feet and reeling from what had happened, needed to see Gene. Sharon had had her problems with Gene in the past, she saw him as destructive and a little scary and a bad influence on Eddie, but she also knew that Gene loved Eddie like she did. She knew that Gene would understand the pain she was feeling, the massive, gaping hole in her life, so she went along to

Sharon recovers in St Martin's Hospital in Bath following the crash.

the show. Billy Fury led Sharon out onto a brightly lit stage that night and the place erupted. Sharon cried through her standing ovation, she cried as the faces in the crowd stared up at her and cried with her and wished her nothing but love and shared in her sorrow. She made her way from the stage to see Gene, hearing voices, no, hearing a single voice, Gene's voice, as she approached his dressing room. Gene was alone, and he was talking to Eddie. He was asking Eddie which pants he should wear for the gig, whether he should wear the blue shirt or not, but Eddie wasn't there to reply. Sharon never went in to the dressing room, she left Gene to deal with his pain his own way, and she went off to deal with hers. Part of Sharon's method of coping with the hurt was the pain pills she began to take and the booze she began to swallow them down with.

Any bad habits that Gene Vincent had accrued in the years leading up to Eddie's death were amplified and intensified following the accident that stole his friend from him. Gene spent just three days in the UK hospital recovering from his injuries before leaving and heading back home for a while. While there, Gene didn't make Eddie's funeral, probably for the same reasons that Johnny Rook couldn't attend, because saying goodbye to Eddie like that would make it real. Gene headed back to the UK and completed Larry Parnes's tour and any expectations that he might not put in a stellar show were quickly dashed when it became obvious that Gene Vincent was leaving everything he had out on the stage every night. The audience needed Gene on those gigs every bit as much as he needed them. The reasoning behind continuing and renaming the tour may have seemed callous to some but for others it provided their chance to get together and say goodbye to Eddie. Fevers were running high by the time the tour got to Liverpool and the gig ended in a riot, a huge pressure release of anger and frustration and sadness that Eddie was gone. The audience that night contained members of The Beatles, soaking up Gene's showmanship and his realness and sharing in his heartbreak.

Eddie died as the 1960s dawned, the decade we are consistently told was a golden age. The new decade brought with it a new generation with their own sound, rock'n'roll turned into the beat boom and splintered off in a thousand different directions from there. Because Eddie had spent so much of his time writing, arranging and recording music, there was much which wasn't released over his lifetime but which, over the coming years, saw the light of day which meant that for his fans, there was still new material to look forward to from their idol. Even though Eddie Cochran was dead, his music wasn't. Eddie had been cutting records for himself and others since 1955. The quality of studios he worked in improved over the course of his career, he got to be able to learn how they worked by putting in the effort. Eddie didn't just turn up and plug in and play, he was there for the whole process and way ahead of the game. The coming decades would bear testimony to just how forward thinking Eddie was as bands such as the Beach Boys and The Beatles

Eddie's funeral at Forest Lawn Cemetery in Cypress on 25 April 1960. Amongst the mourners are Eddie's parents Frank and Alice, Gloria and her son Ed Julson, Eddie's brother Bob and Ritchie Valens' mother Concepcion Valenzuela.

carried on his work, using the studio as a tool and redefining the recording process as they went. If Eddie was in the studio and something needed to be played, he'd play it. The Eddie Cochran Gretsch 6120 sound might have given him away if he was adding guitars to something, but Eddie might have been playing drums, or piano, or he might have been teasing jazz from his Gretsch, or pop, or country. He might have been singing backing vocals or playing his ukulele. Eddie's time as musician for hire held him in good stead. It allowed him the time in the studio he loved so much, to further become enchanted with its possibilities. It also widened his musical knowledge and experience base as he took every opportunity that presented itself to get involved. As a result, a comprehensive list of what Eddie played on is a very tough thing to pin down, session fees were paid in cash and nothing needed to be signed so there's a chance that there is still yet more undiscovered Eddie Cochran music out there. The music he did leave is as potent as it ever was and is still turning people on to rock'n'roll decades after it was recorded. Somewhere in the world right now, someone is sitting on a bed or a couch with a guitar on their lap, learning the chords to 'Summertime Blues'.

As the 1970s turned into the 1980s, twenty years after the tragedy that took Eddie, three young rockabillies flew into London. The trip was the roll of a furry dice inspired by articles they'd read in English music magazines and snippets they'd heard on the radio. They'd heard the rumours of a rockabilly revival starting to take shape in England and thought that their band, the Stray Cats, might do better there than they were in the US. They'd heard that there was a Teddy Boy revival happening in the UK too, alongside the mod revival and the burgeoning new wave scene, and it felt like they might find a home there. Recounting the event years later, Slim Jim Phantom, the Stray Cats' wild man stand-up drummer, recalled how the London that he, Lee Rocker and Brian Setzer landed in was a sea of different tribes, each defined by their haircuts, their clothing, the music they listened to and who their enemies were. Slim Jim said that the one thing that the punks, psychobillies, mods, Teds and rockers from Shepherd's Bush to Camden all had in common, the thing that united them, was that they all dug Eddie Cochran.

The dice rolled lucky and London took to the Cats, the UK liked their punk edge and their purist roots, they liked their rantin' 'n' ravin', their exaggerated pompadours and their cut-off bowling shirts. Word spread about the band quickly, suddenly there were members of Led Zeppelin or the Stones in the audience and the offer of a deal and an album. They recorded their first album with Dave Edmunds producing in 1981, all the while still telling anyone who'd listen that one of the reasons they'd become a band in the first place was Eddie Cochran. Brian Setzer, lead guitarist and singer for the band, was all in on Eddie. He played a 6120, a 1959 model, and just in case there was any doubt, on side one track four was the track 'Jeanie, Jeanie, Jeanie', slightly reworked so that Brian got to say what Eddie was really thinking. In an interview with some long forgotten TV show, Brian Setzer looks straight into the camera and lays out what it is about Eddie. He starts by holding up the 6120 on his lap, "He's it. He's my main man. The guy that really influenced me the most was Eddie Cochran."

The Stray Cats went on to parlay their initial success in London into a career that spanned decades, never losing sight of who'd inspired them to get there. A lot had happened in the twenty years between Eddie's last night on Earth and the Stray Cats touching down in London. The Beatles and the Stones had happened, mods had happened, rockers had happened, hippies had happened, punk had happened and heavy rock had happened. But it seems like if you look closely at all the new heads that the rock'n'roll Hydra grew, you can find some Eddie everywhere. The list of artists who have covered Eddie Cochran songs is a who's who of some of the most seminal figures in recent cultural history. He's in The Beatles' genesis story and The Sex Pistols' *Great*

Rock'n'Roll Swindle, and way more people know his songs than know his name. Over the years, musicians have dug into their past for the songs that touched them, the songs that they mimed to in front of the bedroom mirror and practised over and over, and there's Eddie. There's Eddie's simplicity and his universality. There's his ordinariness and his otherworldliness, there's his celebrity and his everyday guy feel, his closeness to us, his distance.

Roger Daltry of The Who, while introducing his band's live version of 'Summertime Blues' told the crowd that it was the only song we do by another composer, so you bet your life it's good. The Who had survived the sixties, become the loudest band in the world and produced the all-time classic British teen movie *Quadrophenia*, so influential that it helped kickstart a mod revival. They'd sold millions, earned millions and spent a chunk of it covering the bill for the hotel rooms and guitars they trashed along the way. But at the height of it all, when they were one of the biggest bands in the world, renowned for their crafted song writing and embrace of sonic experimentation, they took a moment to share where they came from, and they tipped their cap to Eddie Cochran.

The Who's embrace of Eddie hadn't come from nowhere, the UK had never really let Eddie's death get in the way of its love for him and if anything, it had quietly grown. Showaddywaddy, an almost but not quite UK Teddy Boy band, hit the charts with 'Three Steps to Heaven' in 1975 just as, on London's Kings Road, Malcolm McLaren and Vivienne Westwood were selling clothes inspired by the original British take on rock'n'roll and looking for a band to wear them. They found their band and called them the Sex Pistols. The Pistols' career was a short lived cultural explosion of filth and fury, one of their last singles, just before their inevitable demise, was their version of 'C'Mon Everybody'.

In the UK, Glam Rock hit big in the seventies too, after The Beatles and before punk. Glam took liberally from what had gone before, it pimped it up and pantomimed it and covered it all in glitter. At its height, Marc Bolan and T-Rex took 'Summertime Blues' and jammed it slow until they came up with their bongo-space rock take on the tune. Marc Bolan had been a big fan of Eddie's since he was 13 years old, when he carried Eddie's guitar to his cab for him after the gig at the Finsbury Park Empire. He liked perfect rock'n'roll singles and just in case there was any confusion as to his influences, his Gibson was repainted orange as a nod in Eddie's direction. Marc's career echoed Eddie's in other ways too. Never considered an 'albums' band, Marc Bolan and T-Rex left behind a brace of fabulous, era-defining singles, they experimented with sound and image and saw show-business for what it is, a fabulous and dumb distraction that means everything. In the US in 1975, prog rockers UFO recorded a proto-heavy metal version of 'C'Mon Everybody' that lasted for six and a half minutes at Record Plant Studios for a local radio station.

Over in LA, a guitarist called Joan Jett was playing guitar in The Runaways, the all-girl punk pop band managed by Kim Fowley, the dark Svengali and mischief maker with his own ties to Eddie. The Runaways were around when punk hit LA, Joan got on board with all of it and spray painted her T-shirts to prove her allegiance. When The Runaways broke up, Joan formed a new band and called them The Blackhearts. Armed with her brand new Blackhearts, she tore into 'Summertime Blues' and turned it into a power pop stomper. Joan's version showed that Eddie wasn't just singing for the guys, that the experiences and feelings he captured, the frustration and the angst, the joy and the desire, weren't just a dude thing. Joan meant every word she was singing.

Musical tributes to Eddie in the form of cover versions started to come thick and fast. Bruce Springsteen and the E-Street Band started opening shows with 'Summertime Blues', setting out their stall early. The band had as much fun with the tune as Eddie did, with Little Steven chiming in and the horn section punching home the timeless, perfect riff. Eddie Van Halen, one of the most influential guitarists of his generation, a rock virtuoso compared to classical composers as often as he was to his peers recorded a version of 'Summertime Blues'. When Jimi Hendrix, widely acknowledged as one of, if not the, greatest rock'n'roll guitarists of all time, was celebrated at his funeral they needed music. One of the tunes they chose was Eddie's. Appearing on the *Desert Island Discs* radio show to share the songs which had influenced and formed him, Led Zeppelin's Robert Plant kicked off proceedings with the first rock'n'roll song Eddie cut as a vocalist, 'Pink Peg Slacks'. When Tom Petty and the Heartbreakers were deciding which of their influences to honour, they decided on a cover of 'Somethin' Else'. Rod Stewart, who got his start in the aftermath of the initial burst of rock'n'roll, recorded a version of 'Cut Across Shorty' for his *Gasoline Alley* album, featuring Ronnie Wood on guitar. The tradition of keeping Eddie close is carved in musical stone now. Rock'n'roll musician and obsessive Sonny West plays Eddie's tunes on his huge collection of vintage Gretschs and Sheffield's Richard Hawley loves Eddie, waxing lyrical about his influence, about how a steel worker's son from Sheffield still relates to a singer who died before he was born. On tour in the nineties, in a red Hawaiian shirt and matching lavender T-shirt and pants, Mick Jagger led the Stones through a version of 'Twenty Flight Rock' in Hampton Virginia. Ronnie Wood was front and centre for the solo. By that point the Stones had been the biggest band in the world for what seemed like forever. They'd begun as part of the wave of bands who'd rushed through the doors opened by Eddie and his fellow rock'n'rollers and proceeded to push it as far as it would go, inventing many of the cliches now associated with it along the way. Once again, all the fame and money in the world couldn't stop them turning back to Eddie, introducing him to some people, re-introducing him to others, and paying their respects to one of the greatest there ever was.

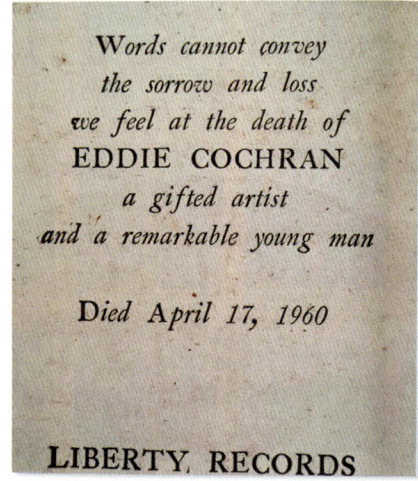

Words cannot convey the sorrow and loss we feel at the death of EDDIE COCHRAN a gifted artist and a remarkable young man

Died April 17, 1960

LIBERTY RECORDS

A Tribute To The Beloved Eddie Cochran
By His Brother Bob

Heavenly music filled the air, that very tragic day.
Something seemed to be missing tho; so I heard the
Creator say;
"We need a master guitar 1st & singer, I know of but
one alone".
"His name is Eddie Cochran." "I think I'll call
him home".

"I know the folks on earth wont mind, for they
will understand, that the Lord loves perfection,
Now we'll have a perfect band."

So as we go through life; now we know, that
perfection is our goal.
And we strive for this; so when we are called;
we'll feel free to go.

"If mere words can console us for the loss of our
beloved Eddie, then our love for him was
a false love."

Written May 6, 1960
By Bob Cochran
Dedicated to all of Eddie's Family and Friends

The Official
BRITISH PAUL ANKA FAN CLUB

Hon. President: PAUL ANKA
President & Secretary: CAROLE WARD

24 WHITEHOUSE ROAD, SHEFFIELD 6, ENGLAND

24th April, 1960.

Dear Mr. & Mrs. Cochran & family,

Through this letter, the members of the 'Paul Anka Fan Club' and myself, and I also speak on behalf of <u>all</u> 'Eddie's' British fans, send our deepest sympathy of the sudden and tragic death of your son Eddie, which happened nr. Bath in England last Sunday 16th instant.

I do understand how upset you all must be over there, and I only hope that you don't mind me sending this letter onto you. I just had to. I tell you, we all over here are awfully upset about this too. Never have I been so unhappy. I just cannot believe this has happened. Why did it have to be Eddie – he was such a marvellous person. Believe me, we will <u>never</u> ever forget him. He was the <u>GREATEST</u>! I would like to take this opportunity of telling you what a wonderful son you had. If I may say so, I will introduce myself to you :– As you can see I run the 'Paul Anka Fan Club' over here in England. (Eddie had just become the Honarary Member of our Club)

Eddie and Paul have always been my favourites, and you can imagine how <u>excited</u> I

"A TRIBUTE TO EDDIE COCHRAN"

He was the greatest American rock 'n' roll star, that today's Teenagers ever knew,
His hair was blond and shiney, his eyes were bright and blue,
His voice, his looks, his personality, had brought him here to fame,
Oh! boy, he was the mostest - Eddie Cochran was his name,
When Eddie visited our fair land, a friend I sure did find,
Gosh! he was so kind to me, it sure will be impossible to find another of his kind,
His act was shown from Sheffield to Bristol, where all his fans went crazy,
With "C'mon Everybody" and that famous shake of the shoulder, he sent the girls all hazy!
Never no more will we see this young man, who caused such a great sensation,
But he will be remembered by us all as a 'Great performer, person and friend; and the same in every nation.

By: Miss. Carole Ward.

"EDDIE COCHRAN DIED IN MY ARMS"
PHOTOPLA

You'll want this memorial tribute to Eddie.

ing as a Waikiki breeze.... The memorial album, "**Eddie Cochran**," is one you'll want to treasure as a memento of a wonderful, talented boy. It includes five tunes Eddie wrote himself. (For **Shari Sheeley**'s story of the tragic accident in which Eddie was killed, just before they were to be married, turn to page 32).... **Dinah** and

EDDIE COCHRAN 32   "Eddie Died in My Arms"   by Marcia Borie
and SHARI SHEELEY

Shari Sheeley:

"Eddie told me: 'Something awful's going to happen. I can feel it. You'll never be Mrs. Cochran.' And then,

EDDIE DIED IN MY ARMS

only two hours later. I still can't believe it.

(Continued on page 76)

32

EDDIE COCHRAN

The truth about the late
EDDIE COCHRAN
By his fiancée, Sharon Sheeley

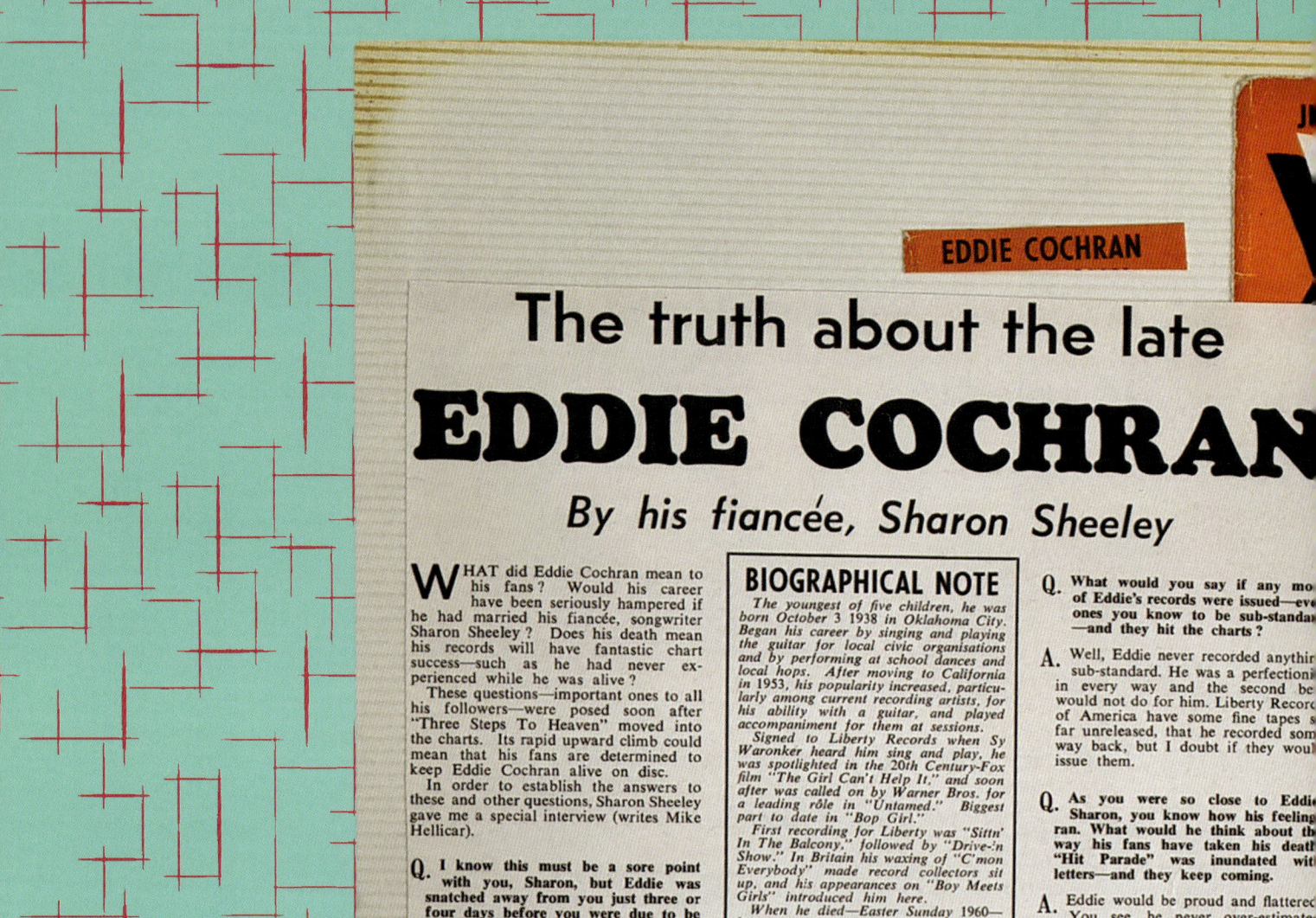

WHAT did Eddie Cochran mean to his fans? Would his career have been seriously hampered if he had married his fiancée, songwriter Sharon Sheeley? Does his death mean his records will have fantastic chart success—such as he had never experienced while he was alive?

These questions—important ones to all his followers—were posed soon after "Three Steps To Heaven" moved into the charts. Its rapid upward climb could mean that his fans are determined to keep Eddie Cochran alive on disc.

In order to establish the answers to these and other questions, Sharon Sheeley gave me a special interview (writes Mike Hellicar).

Q. I know this must be a sore point with you, Sharon, but Eddie was snatched away from you just three or four days before you were due to be married. Do you think, had he lived, he would have wanted the marriage kept secret?

A. No, not my Eddie. You see, he hated anything secret or underground, and refused to deceive anyone over anything—no matter how small. Don't worry about hurting my feelings over mentioning the marriage, for I'm still so close to Eddie I feel that we were married.

Q. Do you think that Eddie's popularity rating would have dropped once it was learnt that he had married?

A. Not in the least. Eddie was very close to his fans, and could never do enough for them. He loved them all, and they loved him. I have been receiving forty letters a day from people who are not only his fans, but just those who read about the accident—and everyone sympathises with me for not being able to marry such a swell guy.

Q. Do you think "Three Steps To Heaven" would have been a chart success for Eddie even if he had not died?

A. Without doubt Eddie's death has made no difference. We knew right from the recording session that it was going to be a hit, and it was no surprise to me to see the record climb.

BIOGRAPHICAL NOTE
The youngest of five children, he was born October 3 1938 in Oklahoma City. Began his career by singing and playing the guitar for local civic organisations and by performing at school dances and local hops. After moving to California in 1953, his popularity increased, particularly among current recording artists, for his ability with a guitar, and played accompaniment for them at sessions.

Signed to Liberty Records when Sy Waronker heard him sing and play, he was spotlighted in the 20th Century-Fox film "The Girl Can't Help It," and soon after was called on by Warner Bros. for a leading role in "Untamed." Biggest part to date in "Bop Girl."

First recording for Liberty was "Sittin' In The Balcony," followed by "Drive-'n Show." In Britain his waxing of "C'mon Everybody" made record collectors sit up, and his appearances on "Boy Meets Girls" introduced him here.

When he died—Easter Sunday 1960—he was on his way to London Airport with Sharon, stage partner and close friend Gene Vincent, and show manager Pat Thompkins.

Q. What would you say if any mo[re] of Eddie's records were issued—eve[n] ones you know to be sub-standa[rd] —and they hit the charts?

A. Well, Eddie never recorded anythin[g] sub-standard. He was a perfectioni[st] in every way and the second be[st] would not do for him. Liberty Record[s] of America have some fine tapes s[o] far unreleased, that he recorded som[e] way back, but I doubt if they woul[d] issue them.

Q. As you were so close to Eddie Sharon, you know how his feeling[s] ran. What would he think about th[e] way his fans have taken his death[.] "Hit Parade" was inundated wit[h] letters—and they keep coming.

A. Eddie would be proud and flattered[.] You see, he never over-estimate[d] himself, and regarded any break tha[t] came his way as a piece of luck tha[t] was controlled by someone else. A[s] Eddie cannot know of the way hi[s] death was received, I am passing on al[l] letters to his mother, and she wil[l] treasure them, for she was so prou[d] of her son.

Q. Do you think Eddie would want to be mourned in the same way a[s] Buddy Holly still is?

A. That's a difficult question, for Eddie and Buddy were the best of pals, and it came as a tremendous shock to Eddie when his friend died in that fateful plane crash. I do know he would feel highly complimented to be put on the same par as Buddy.

Q. Anything special you would like to say to Hit Parade readers about Eddie?

A. On his family's behalf, I would like to thank readers for the wonderful letters and gifts that have poured in. I think Eddie's fans are unique, because they have stayed so loyal to him, and once they knew he and I were engaged, they immediately accepted me into their circle.

Everyone has been so wonderful, and you can be sure that if it is at all possible, his mother will know about every letter, gift and phone call I had.

Little Richard, Alis Lesley and Eddie publicising their Australian tour.

Where are they now?

Chuck Berry

CHUCK ENDED UP serving some jail time for the charges levelled against him as the 1950s drew to a close. Upon his release in 1963, the musical landscape was changing yet again and the new wave of bands, led by The Beatles and the Stones, were proudly declaring Chuck Berry as a founding influence. The Stones were even covering his tunes, throwing in some James Brown moves and a little London swagger and introducing him to the kids all over again. His personal and professional life continued as a rollercoaster of ups and down until his death in 2017 at the age of 90. As the years passed, the acknowledgement of his influence and importance only grew. Before long they were calling Chuck Berry the Father of rock'n'roll and his legacy was secure, so secure that when they were deciding which music to send up to space on Voyager One, they decided upon Chuck's 'Johnny B. Goode'. Chuck received a Grammy Lifetime Achievement Award, was honoured with an eight-foot tall animatronic statue in St Louis and named one of the greatest of all time by *Rolling Stone* magazine. At Chuck's funeral, a Cherry Red Gibson lay alongside him in his coffin.

Joe Brown

JOE BROWN'S CAREER was only just beginning when he met Eddie Cochran on *The Fast Moving Beat Show*. The chirpy cockney with the Gibson and the leather jacket went on to appear in six movies, present radio shows for the BBC and star in a West End theatre show. The tricks that Eddie taught Joe as they rehearsed for *The Fast Moving Beat Show* stood Joe in good stead and he never forgot his American friend.

Johnny Burnette

JOHNNY CONTINUED TO record for Liberty, for a while, following the death of his friend and label-mate, before signing to two other records label and finally starting his own, Sahara. Just four years after the crash that killed Eddie, in August 1964, Johnny was out fishing at night with no lights on his boat when it was rammed by a cabin cruiser. Johnny didn't survive the accident which occurred, spookily, in Clear Lake, California. Johnny's music lived on though. The rockers and the Teddy Boys never forgot him, The Beatles covered his tune 'Lonesome Tears In My Eyes', the Yardbirds did a killer version of 'Train Kept A Rollin'', Ringo Starr covered 'You're Sixteen', then The Cramps reintroduced Johnny to the punk rock crowd with their torn up version of 'Tear It Up'. If you talk about rockabilly and rock'n'roll, at some point you'll talk about Johnny Burnette.

Jerry Capehart

THANKS TO HIS time with Eddie, Jerry Capehart's name appears as co-writer on some of the most iconic and important tunes in rock'n'roll history. The year after the crash, Jerry had another hit on his hands when Glen Campbell scored his first hit with 'Turn Around, Look at Me'. Jerry put out a 45, 'Song of New Orleans' on Crest Records in 1962. Jerry gave himself full performance credit on the tune despite the fact that it was 'Fourth Man Theme', a demo that Eddie had made and played every instrument on. A dealmaker 'til the end, when he died from cancer in Nashville in 1998, Jerry was in the midst of pitching his latest musical idea, a song called 'Summertime Blues No. 2'.

Jeanne Carmen

JEANNE'S LIFE HAD been extraordinary before she knew Eddie, and continued to be so after he passed. Jeanne had to cut short her career as model, actress and trick-shot golf hustler when she was ordered to leave Hollywood by 'Handsome' Johnny Rosselli, one of mob-boss Sam Giancana's right hand men. The order was prompted by the death of starlet turned Goddess, Marilyn Monroe. Whatever Jeanne knew, or whatever she thought people thought she knew, was enough to convince her to hightail it to Scottsdale, Arizona, live a quiet life well away from the spotlight and her old pursuits and never publicly talk about her past. Jeanne died in 2007, survived by her three children. The epitaph on her headstone reads 'She Came, She Saw, She Conquered.'

Dick Clark

DICK CLARK'S AMERICAN *Bandstand*, the show that put so many early rock'n'rollers on TV, often for the first time, ran until 1989. Alongside his musical shows, such as *Dick Clark's Saturday Beech-Nut Show*, where Eddie appeared three times, Clark rang in the New Year on his *Dick Clark's New Year's Rockin' Eve*, broadcast every 31 December live from Times Square in New York. Upon his death in Santa Monica in 2012, Clark was recognised not only for his contribution to the popularity of the music he championed but also for his services to racial integration and his early, inclusive approach to programming. Among those who praised Dick for his cultural contribution were Diana Ross, Berry Gordy and President Obama.

Hank Cochran

THERE WERE NO hard feelings between Hank and Eddie at the demise of The Cochran Brothers. When the band split and Eddie went one way and Hank another, the two remained friendly and Hank would later recall the last time he saw Eddie, when Eddie was starting to find his feet as a solo artist and find success on his own terms. Eddie turned up at Hank's place with beers and a smile, looking to hang out and celebrate and wish each other luck for the future. They toasted each other and hugged and Hank never saw Eddie again. Hank Cochran continued the journey and inevitably, all roads led to Nashville, the capital of country, where he carved out the career he had always been destined for.

Joe Cocker

JOE COCKER, WHO watched Eddie from the good seats down front, had a voice built for raucous, rocky blues that took him all the way to festival spots at Woodstock and the Isle of Wight. Joe hit the top of the UK charts in 1968 with his cover of The Beatles' 'With a Little Help From My Friends' and won a Grammy in 1983 for his movie-song duet with Jennifer Warnes, 'Up Where We Belong'. Joe Cocker made a total of twenty-two albums before his death in 2014, he is commemorated in his home town of Sheffield with a bronze plaque and was awarded an OBE for Services to Music in 2007.

Sandra Dee

SHORTLY AFTER THEY spent the day working together, Eddie's audition partner Sandra Dee went on to become one of the biggest movie stars in America. She is now probably most fondly remembered for her lead role in *Gidget*, and for the gentle teasing she received in the musical *Grease*. As the 1960s progressed and tastes changed, the desire to see the kind of wholesome beach party movies and toothless romantic comedies that Dee was famous for declined and the offers started coming in less and less. Sandra Dee would later regret the wholesome image she'd adopted, saying that it was foisted on her by movie execs and Hollywood publicists who, when she was in public, would regularly snatch cigarettes from her hands and cover her cocktails with napkins.

Fats Domino

THE QUIET, UNASSUMING Fats, real name Antoine Dominique Domino Jr, went on to sell over a 100 million records during his long career and was amongst the first names inducted into the Rock'n'Roll Hall of Fame. So respected was Fats by his peers that when Elvis first met Fats Domino in 1959, he declared him the real King of rock'n'roll.

Mamie Van Doren

AFTER WORKING WITH Eddie on *Untamed Youth*, Mamie earned her crown as Queen of the B-movies with a string of low budget drive-in classics. She hung out with The Beatles and was romantically linked with Steve McQueen, Howard Hughes, Clint Eastwood, Burt Reynolds and Clark Gable.

Vince Eager

VINCE WAS SHATTERED by Eddie's death. The two had bonded while they worked together and become friends. Unaware that the crash had happened, Vince waited for Eddie at the airport he was heading toward but of course, Eddie never showed up. Vince kept performing, played the lead role in the musical *Elvis!*, and is still recording and releasing records with some of his fellow Larry Parnes's stablemates.

Adam Faith

FOLLOWING HIS EMERGENCE as an early British rocker, Adam Faith, unlike some of his contemporaries, managed to stay both relevant and popular as the 1960s changed the cultural landscape. Seven of Adam's singles found a spot in the Top 5 and following his early acting experience, in the movie *Beat Girl*, he went on to find fame as a TV actor in the show *Budgie*. As well as music and acting, Adam also took up journalism, specialising in financial matters. Adam died in 2003.

Georgie Fame

GEORGIE FAME WENT on to carve a career at the keyboards which lasted for decades. In the mid-60s, Georgie released his floor-filler Brit beat take on 'Yeh, Yeh', and in 1967 scored a Top 10 hit on both sides of the Atlantic with 'The Ballad of Bonnie and Clyde'. Held in the highest regard by his contemporaries and those who followed, Georgie Fame is still playing and recording.

Kim Fowley

KIM FOWLEY'S CAREER blossomed, albeit weirdly, in the 1960s, when he collaborated on and produced a string of off-kilter classics by acts such as Frank Zappa and The Mothers of Invention and, in 1969, Gene Vincent. Fowley went on to produce Jonathan Richman and The Modern Lovers, write songs with Kiss and manage The Runaways, the tough as hell LA girl group featuring Joan Jett and Lita Ford. As well as his music, in later life Kim worked as an experimental film-maker and writer. After a fifty-plus year career in the music industry, Kim Fowley died in 2015, aged 75.

Alan Freed

A COUPLE OF years after Eddie's death the Payola scandal caught up with Alan Freed when he was proven to have taken payments and charged with counts of commercial bribery. Freed 'fessed up and paid the fine but his career took a hit as a result and never reached its early, heady heights. Freed got hit with a huge tax bill he couldn't cover and was effectively blacklisted within the industry before his death in 1965. When the dust settled, and people started to look seriously at the early days of rock'n'roll, Freed's contribution, the role he played in getting the music on radio and the silver screen, was undeniable. Freed was posthumously honoured with a star on the Hollywood Walk of Fame and induction into the Rock'n'Roll Hall of Fame and his films are still the best way to see many early rockers, boppers and bluesmen in action.

Billy Fury

BILLY FURY'S STAR kept on shining following the *Fast Moving Beat Show*. Over the coming decade he racked up as many hits as The Beatles and his tunes spent a total of 332 weeks on the UK charts. Billy branched out into acting and, ten years before his death, gave a stellar performance playing alongside David Essex in the 1973 rockstar classic, *That'll Be The Day*.

Eddie's guitar

FOLLOWING THE CRASH, Eddie's 6120, the guitar he'd bought from Bell Gardens Music Centre and made his own, was returned to Alice at the family home at Buena Park. Shrimper put the guitar in Eddie's room with his clothes, records guns and knives and let few people enter the shrine she'd built to her youngest child. Inevitably, Shrimper struggled to come to terms with her son's death and for a while dealt with her loss with denial, by convincing herself that Eddie was just away and that he'd soon be back, laughing with his mother again, regaling her with his adventures and tucking into her cornbread and beans. Eddie's guitar is now on display at the Rock'n'Roll Hall of Fame in Cleveland Ohio along with Eddie's stage clothes from his appearance at the 1960 *NME* Poll Winners Party in Wembley.

Guybo

Guybo lived long enough to see the friend he'd made back in Bell Gardens, the one he spent countless hours learning, playing and recording music with, become a legend. It's impossible to talk about Eddie without talking about Guybo, it's impossible to talk about the Eddie Cochran sound without paying tribute to Guybo, and due to his inclusion on Eddie's iconic live forever recordings, Guybo is impossible to forget. He became active on social media in later life, happily interacting with fans old and new, a last living link to Eddie. Connie 'Guybo' Smith died during the writing of this book, on 4 February 2023.

Lee Hazlewood

FOLLOWING HIS WORK with Duane Eddy and Eddie Cochran in the late 1950s, Lee Hazlewood went on to develop his own psychedelic country sound and produced some of the 1960s' finest moments with Nancy Sinatra. Lee set up his own label and signed Gram Parsons' first group, The International Submarine Band. When Parsons left to join the Byrds and took his material with him to record *Sweetheart of the Rodeo*, a big legal bust up ensued. But Lee Hazlewood was an artist, not a businessman. Lee died in 2007.

Jerry Lee Lewis

JERRY LEE CONTINUED to live in the purgatory between righteous and evil driven by fire, booze, and brimstone. The Killer, as he came to be known, once got so wasted he turned up at the gates to Graceland brandishing a pistol and demanding to see Elvis. Though his marriage to his young cousin was never quite forgiven or forgotten, he did live long enough to see the work he'd done way back then gain the serious recognition it deserved. Jerry Lee got a star on the Hollywood Walk of Fame, a place at the top table of the Rock'n'Roll Hall of Fame and was a wildman to the end. Jerry Lee Lewis died in 2022.

Jayne Mansfield

WITH A CAREER that spanned twenty-three movies, the Playmate turned movie star Jayne Mansfield's on-screen presence and off-screen lifestyle ensured that she would forever be remembered. Jayne got married three times and had five children and was at one point romantically linked to Bobby Kennedy. In 1966, while in San Francisco to attend a film festival, Jayne visited The Church of Satan to meet with its founder, Anton Lavey. During the visit, Lavey bestowed Jayne with the title 'High Priestess of San Francisco's Church of Satan' and presented her with a medallion to mark the occasion. Jayne Mansfield died in 1967, at the age of 34, in a car wreck in Louisiana.

George Martin

THE 19-YEAR-OLD DRIVER of the cab that Eddie died in was charged with causing death by dangerous driving. His case was heard on the 23 and 24 June 1960 at Bristol Assizes where he was found guilty of causing the accident by travelling at excessive speed, disqualified from driving, fined fifty pounds and warned that if he didn't pay it he'd serve six months in prison. George paid the fine.

Larry Parnes

LARRY PARNES STAYED in the entertainment industry although as time passed, his focus shifted. The 1960s beat boom wiped out the acts Larry had spent so long cultivating and he no longer had his finger on the pulse of pop music. He turned his attention to theatre and managing a world class ice-skater, where he was successful enough to maintain his race horses and the lifestyle he had become accustomed to. His reputation for keeping an eye on the bottom line was celebrated prior to Eddie's arrival in the UK when he received the nickname 'Mr Parnes, Shillings and Pence'. He retired from show business in 1981 and died eight years later.

Eddie in the front yard
of 5539 Priory Street
in Bell Gardens.

Sam Phillips

SAMUEL CORNELIUS PHILLIPS kept going and made his fortune. He left the label he founded and ran Sun Records, with a back catalogue that contains some of the most important music ever recorded. The Million Dollar Quartet all went on to live up to their name and helped Sam change popular music forever. Sam has been inducted into just about every musical Hall of Fame there is and, fittingly, Sun Studios is now a National Historic Landmark.

Elvis Presley

BY THE TIME Eddie Cochran died, Elvis Presley was the fully anointed King of Rock'n'Roll, a title which remains incontestable to this day. When he died in 1977, Elvis had made countless movies and albums and was one of the most recognisable faces on planet Earth. Elvis Presley still informs the culture and seventy years on since he started cutting records, audiences are still discovering them.

Jack Ruby

TEXAS CLUB OWNER Jack will be forever remembered as the man who shot Lee Harvey Oswald with his Colt Cobra .38 as Oswald was being questioned by police and government agencies about his part in the assassination of President John F. Kennedy. No real answer exists as to why Jack did what he did but conspiracies abound. Whatever secrets Jack was keeping he took to the grave with him when he died in mysterious circumstances, having just been paid a visit by a doctor with ties to shady government MK Ultra.

Sharon Sheeley

IT TOOK A while, but Sharon eventually recovered from the injuries she sustained in the crash. Despite going on to fulfil her early potential and carve a solid career for herself over the coming years, she never forgot Eddie. Sharon created the show *Shindig!* along with Jack Good and her husband, DJ Jimmy O'Neill. Sharon's instincts where television was concerned proved to be as on point as her musical taste, and the show was a hit. When Sharon Sheeley died in 2002, a cenotaph marker was placed to remember her in Forest Memorial Park, where Eddie is buried.

Little Richard

LITTLE RICHARD DIDN'T remain a preacher forever, although his faith remained no matter how much he tested it. His musical influence didn't end with rock'n'roll and coming generations of soul, funk, hip-hip and R'n'B performers would find inspiration in Reverend Richard's wild charisma, his explosive showmanship and his ear for a killer tune. Little Richard died in 2020 but like his fellow founders of rock'n'roll, his legacy is secure.

Phil Spector

BEFORE HE WOUND up in jail, Phil Spector used the lessons he learnt early in his career and went on to invent his own (wall of) sound, define the sixties girl group and leave behind a collection of stone cold classics. Like Eddie, Phil Spector was an early advocate of the possibilities of recorded sound and eventually, rarely left the studio. In the February of 2003, Phil Spector shot and killed Lana Clarkson in his Hollywood home. The shot was heard by Spector's limousine driver who informed the authorities. Spector was arrested, charged, found guilty of the murder and died in prison in 2021.

Surf Ballroom, Clear Lake

AS A TRIBUTE to the passengers and pilot who perished on the flight, a memorial has been erected outside the Surf Ballroom which still retains the same, now vintage, facade. The Surf Ballroom is frozen in time, it looks identical to the venue that Buddy, Ritchie and J.P. pulled up at and is still a point of rock'n'roll pilgrimage to this day. The memorial stone reads:

The above legends played their last concert at The Surf Ballroom, Clearlake, Iowa, on 2 February 1959. Their earthly life tragically ended 5.2 miles northwest of the Mason City Airport, 3 February 1959. Their music lives on.

The Clear Lake tragedy features in 'La Bamba', the Ritchie Valens biopic where Lou Diamond Phillips stars as Ritchie and Brian Setzer plays Eddie. As an adjunct, Eddie's 'Three Stars' isn't the only time music was used to help process the Clear Lake tragedy, Don McLean's song 'American Pie' ensured that the crash would be forever known as the day the music died.

Gene Vincent

GENE HAD DEMONS before his second automobile accident and the loss of Eddie did nothing to soothe them. Speaking on 20 April, Gene said how strange it was not having Eddie around, how he wanted to call out to him. Virtually ignored in his homeland as the 1960s progressed, Europe never forgot Gene and provided him a home and audience during the coming years. The coming years weren't kind to Gene though, he indulged his bad habits and gave mean Gene more and more rein until his death from alcohol related illness in 1971. As with Eddie, Gene Vincent has been rediscovered time and again by generation after generation, 'Be-Bop-a-Lula' is rightly regarded as a rock'n'roll masterpiece and Gene is now viewed with the respect he deserves.

Marty Wilde

MARTY WILDE CARRIED on having hits under his own name and writing them for others, including Status Quo. The next generation of Wilde's, featuring his daughter Kim and her brother Ricky, wrote songs with their dad and had a smash hit with 'Kids In America'.

Pieces of Eddie's clothing, including his hand-tooled belt, from Sonny West's Lost Locker Collection.

Acknowledgements

WHERE EDDIE COCHRAN is concerned, there are a few key books which have each been indispensable in researching this one. Each offers a different perspective on Eddie's life and times and all are worth reading by fans and newcomers alike. A special thanks goes out to the authors.

Don't Forget Me: The Eddie Cochran Story by Julie Mundy and Darrel Higham.
Published by Mainstream.

Don't Forget Me is an exhaustive, in-depth look at the life and career of Eddie Cochran. As well as Eddie's biography the book provides a comprehensive look at the music Eddie made, where and when he made it and who he made it with. The book covers Eddie's life and the backdrop to it while exploring the rise of rock'n'roll and the people who made it.

Three Steps to Heaven: The Eddie Cochran Story by Bobby Cochran and Susan Van Hecke.
Published by Hal Leonard.

Bobby Cochran's book is written from the perspective of Eddie's nephew and offers exclusive insight into his background and family. Three Steps to Heaven relates Eddie's experience to Bobby's own life as a musician and contains a wealth of behind-the-scenes Cochran family stories and secrets. Bobby talks about his own highs and lows and explores the influence of Eddie Cochran on his career and life.

Eddie Cochran: A Fast Moving Beat Show by Adrian McKenna and John Firminger.
Published by Dirty Stopouts.com

A Fast Moving Beat Show is a fully illustrated deep dive into Eddie's final tour of the UK featuring tour schedules and set lists, a detailed look at the UK they were travelling through and interviews with people who caught Eddie and Gene on that final tour. The book explores every aspect of Eddie's last months on the road, the musicians who travelled with him and the cast of new characters who first marvelled at Eddie, and then took him into their hearts.

Heartfelt personal thanks go out to Trudy, Osian and Marcus and to Jon, Libby, Austin, Michael and Claire. Also to Isy at Creative Authors, Caroline at Rupert Crew, to Rob, Anna, Matt and Team Amazing Finds and Dave and Matteo. Huge thanks also to David, Simon, Sonny, Graeme and Greg, and to Betty, Paul, Janine and Thomas Milton Bullman.

Sonny West and Simon Green at Killertone Records would like to thank Graeme Corner, Copied Right and Greg Tiernan.

The publishers would like to thank Isabel Atherton, Lee Bullman, Graeme Corner, Max Décharné, Simon Green and Lora Findlay for all their invaluable help with *Eddie Cochran in Person*. And special thanks to Sonny West, owner of the Lost Locker Collection, for access to such amazing material.

Photo Credits

Page 5 © Sonny West

Page 6, 10, 12–18, 21, 22, 24–8, 29–32, 34–5, 37, 38, 40–1, 43–60, 62–80, 82–88, 90–94, bottom 97, 98–107, 109–115, 117–120, 122–5, 127–134, 137–145, 149, 151, 156–9, 164–177, 184, 186–7, 188, 190–192 © the Eddie Cochran Lost Locker Collection

Page 42 © Michael Ochs Archives

Page 96, 97 © Douglas Kirkland

Page 108 © Hulton Archive/Getty Images

Page 126 © Michael Ochs Archives

Page 146, 162 © Harry Hammond/V&A Images/Getty Images

Page 150 © Michael Ochs Archives

Page 152 © GAB Archive/Getty Images

Page 155 © Michael Ochs Archives

Page 180 © Fairfax Media/Getty Images

Original artwork for the 1960 Liberty Records LP *The Eddie Cochran Memorial Album*.